'DJ Paulette's debut book Welcome to [the club is] a key talent involved in [shaping] our hearts, by way of the music indus[try]'

Jacqueline Springer

'Icon. Trailblazer. Activist. Warrior. DJ Paulette has led the way for Black women and women everywhere in a global music industry riddled with racism and misogyny. She has blown apart the myths. This is a magnificent book. A manifesto for our times and a rallying call for the future.'

Maxine Peake, actor

'Paulette continues to light the way for others, building in relevance and significance, wowing crowds, annihilating dancefloors. I would recommend *Welcome to the club* as an essential read for anyone and everyone. I thoroughly enjoyed it.'

Craig Charles, actor and DJ

'I now realise the weight of the obstacles and challenges Paulette overcame, her fortitude to compete in male-dominated arenas, the racism she undoubtedly encountered. Her mettle and contribution have clearly opened doors for the diversity and equality we strive for today.'

Simon Dunmore, DJ and founder of Defected Records

'Paulette is a pioneer, a ground-breaker, a trailblazer and never afraid to hold a mirror up to the world to show that there is still so much more to do. A self-assured shimmy of a book that instantly transports you to the dancefloor and beyond. I love it!'

Arielle Free, DJ and radio presenter

'When I met Paulette, back in early 1990s Manchester, I don't think any of us understood what we were getting out of nightlife beyond raw enjoyment. Now we've had a chance to re-evaluate those codes, to understand how much they meant in forming us. This book explains why nightlife matters. Paulette understands the philosophy of the nightclub, because she was there when it was at its very best.'

Paul Flynn, author of *Good as You*

'Paulette has experienced the highs and lows of dance music culture. This heartfelt book tells the story of what she saw and learned with her distinctive style, warmth and wicked wit.'

Matthew Collin, author of *Rave On*

'Paulette is someone I've always respected, admired and been inspired by. This book is beautifully written, incisive, dry, witty and real – true Mancunian honesty. What an adventure and a truly fascinating life.'
Rowetta, singer

'With fierce resilience and passion, DJ Paulette's travels through clubland reveal her personal triumphs over life's adversities. A book filled with music and love, positivity and enthusiasm.'
Princess Julia, DJ and writer

'DJ Paulette turns notable moments in her thirty-year career into a close listening experience. There's a musical quality to this book that sounds like what Black women DJs have tried to tell the world – our unique experiences turn any party into a lively classroom. Paulette leaves curious readers waiting for the next chapter so they can hear it like a song.'
Lynnée Denise, DJ and scholar

'DJ Paulette's essential read doubles up as an alternative history of dance music, told from the middle of the dancefloor. It's a sparkling ride through high times and low, documenting racism, sexism and homophobia with fabulous clarity. A full-bodied celebration of the ways music can save your life – and can also make your life.'
Emma Warren, author of *Dance Your Way Home*

'Any list of the pioneers of the Manchester club scene is not complete without the name DJ Paulette. We are so proud of her.'
Andy Burnham, Mayor of Greater Manchester

'I arrived in 1990s Manchester, found a place to live and a job then got dragged up, went clubbing and there was DJ Paulette on the decks. Her energy and music were the soundtrack to my queer gender-bending dance floor years. If music and clubbing played an important part in your life, then so will this book.'
Kate O'Donnell, actor, writer and maker

'Written with warmth and passion, this book continues the trend of female professionals telling their stories – the good and the bad ones – so that we learn how clubs can once again become places of peace, love, unity and respect.'
Beate Peter, The Lapsed Clubber Project

Welcome to the club

Manchester University Press

Welcome to the club

The life and lessons of a Black woman DJ

DJ Paulette

Manchester University Press

Copyright © DJ Paulette 2024

The right of DJ Paulette to be identified as the author of this work has been asserted in accordance with the Copyright, Designs and Patents Act 1988.

Published by Manchester University Press
Oxford Road, Manchester, M13 9PL

www.manchesteruniversitypress.co.uk

British Library Cataloguing-in-Publication Data
A catalogue record for this book is available from the British Library

ISBN 978 1 5261 6690 6 hardback
ISBN 978 1 5261 8356 9 paperback

First published 2024

The publisher has no responsibility for the persistence or accuracy of URLs for any external or third-party internet websites referred to in this book, and does not guarantee that any content on such websites is, or will remain, accurate or appropriate.

EU authorised representative for GPSR:
Easy Access System Europe – Mustamäe tee 50, 10621 Tallinn, Estonia, gpsr.requests@easproject.com

Typeset
by Cheshire Typesetting Ltd, Cuddington, Cheshire
Printed in the UK by CPI Group (UK) Ltd, Croydon CR0 4YY

Contents

Foreword by Annie Mac   vii

Introduction: welcome to the club
  (Belleville or Bust)   1
1 Finders keepers: in the beginning   16
2 London to Paris: Eurostar   39
3 Bad behaviour: shit shags and crap hotels   72
4 FAQs (female asked questions)   94
5 How to kill a DJ   119
6 Sane as it ever was   142
7 Lifetime VIP: a manifesto   184

Appendix: future forces   210
Discography   213
Acknowledgements   215
List of illustrations   220
Notes   224
Index   240

Foreword

Annie Mac

DJ Paulette is a foremother to all of us, a woman who has tirelessly worked to share her passion for music with the world, and who has become a doyen of DJ culture as a result. Her contributions to electronic music are vast and varied; she has worked in radio stations, record labels, magazines, recording studios and, most powerfully, in DJ booths, where she has been resident DJ in some of the most prestigious clubs in the world. This is an entire life dedicated to clubs and club culture, and now, it's documented.

Welcome to the club is a heartfelt and at times both hilarious and frustrating account of Paulette's own story, spanning the scenes she has inhabited, the characters she has encountered and the many twists and turns and ups and downs of her career. Upon reading it, I felt that all-too-familiar jolt of anger in realising that I have never read a book about dance music culture written by a woman, let alone a woman of colour. DJ Paulette's perspective is totally unique, and therefore invaluable.

Throughout my own career as a DJ, I never felt like I had female role models in DJing. Coming through the radio ranks, I was able to champion and platform the music movements that came and went: the Ed Banger and Justice dance

Foreword

rock explosion, Scream and Benga era dubstep and then a new generation of house superstars with Disclosure at the helm. And in the clubs, as I grew more confident as a DJ and a curator, it was always the same. I was always the only woman on the line-up. In the last decade I have witnessed a slow surge of young female and non-binary DJs coming through the ranks, and seen the industry begin to be held to account for the chronic gender and racial inequality on line-ups, in the charts and in the board rooms. Change has begun, but the pace is glacial. There is still so much work to do.

DJ Paulette has been here for over three decades, a Black queer woman, breaking through the gates of the boys' clubs, enduring the knock-backs and fighting for a seat at the table. A virtuoso when it comes to her craft, she has endured the prejudice, the privilege and the bias of the industry around her to stay true to the communion, unity and utter joy of the dancefloor.

Her story is a vital and vivid document of a remarkable and pioneering career. A career that we should all bear witness to in order to truly understand our beloved dance music culture in the UK. I wish I had met Paulette early on in my career. I wish I could have sat with her and just listened. Now we all get that privilege.

Introduction: welcome to the club (Belleville or Bust)

It's a balmy, Parisian evening in 2011, and I've been on one of my favourite walks past Père Lachaise, that grand city within a cemetery, to meet Gilles Peterson and friends at Mama Shelter.[1] I had been living and DJ'ing in Paris for seven years and, call it loyalty or tradition, whenever Gilles was on the radio I emailed in for a shout out, and if he was in town, I made the trip to see him, Rob Gallagher, Sean Rollins and the Brownswood record label crew. After his set at La Bellevilloise[2] we hung out back in the hotel bar. Our group had fallen into an animated discussion about music and DJ'ing – I was telling some random story about touring in France when Gilles turned, looked at me and said, 'Yeah but – do you still LOVE it?' He scrutinised my face then laughed cheekily. 'You still LOVE it, don't you! When are you going to write that book, eh? – You should read that Anthony Bourdain book – *Kitchen Confidential* ... write something like that.'

I took the hint, bought the book, read it in a couple of days then tried to write something profound but I couldn't find an edge. I had no heavy AAA-list names to drop because I wasn't a regular in the green rooms that mattered. I've had designer handbags and underwear that has lasted longer than my longest relationships and could report only average sex with a series of low-rent, short-stay partners. I had no wild fashion stories and had taken nowhere near enough drugs to qualify as a bankable rehab rescue case. Yet still I wrote. I showed samples of my work to a few people. Laidback Luke told me that most DJs he knew only wanted to make music and didn't read books. It scored *nul points* from my Commissioning Editor friend at Random House who said that he only signed best-selling celebrity titles to his roster. Frank Broughton[3] told me that while he could see I'd got the chops to write, without the sex, drugs and rock and roll it wasn't that interesting really. Deflated, I put my writing dreams to bed.

But Freud writes, 'the repressed will always return', and people say that everyone has one book in them. Freud is right and those pesky people have a point. So here is my story.

I'm DJ Paulette. After thirty years in the business (which is surely long enough to hope that people know that I play records in clubs for a living), I still use the 'DJ' prefix as an aide memoire. Secretly, it bumps me up the listings on alphabetical order line-ups and poster credits but don't tell anybody. Like Madonna, I'm mononymous. I only use my second name in private because it's my surname by marriage, and since I've been divorced for twenty-six years there's no point in giving that side of the story too much oxygen.

This is not a complete history of electronic dance music nor is it a definitive DJ Paulette biography: quite a few places, people and events are missing so don't @ me. It takes a series of snapshots that follow a chronological arc from the start of my DJ'ing career to the present day, bending this through the prism of other people's histories to

Introduction

acknowledge the wider picture. After all, ten people at a party will never tell the same story.

It starts in Manchester in 1992 with its backdrop of the Aids crisis, Section 28, recession, the Poll Tax, the backdraft from the SUS[4] laws, Tim Berners Lee's introduction of the World Wide Web and the completion of the Channel Tunnel; it finishes somewhere in the present after Little Simz and Kendrick Lamarr headlined and closed Glastonbury Festival, after we celebrated fifty years of London Pride, stuck a pin in the moment when Beyoncé's global number one album *Renaissance* dropped to save house music[5] and we lost Queen Elizabeth II (RIP).

I have the unique perspective of an outsider with insider knowledge and an insider with outsider knowledge: opinions and views are my own. The themes, situations and issues have been put into context with the pivotal people I have worked with, for and alongside. These are power-players and decision-makers who were there from the start, who are important contributors today, and who are taking the music industry future forwards to create a diverse and more robust place for us all to work and enjoy without prejudice. I stitch this patchwork together with a little history, some socio-cultural commentary, a splash of politics, and a lot of love. It's a living history; we still have miles to go before we sleep.[6]

Before I became a DJ, I got my first taste of working in the music industry when I was eighteen years old. My Calvin Klein Obsession-soaked application worked, and I was called up to audition as an on-air reporter for the new youth magazine programme called *Saturday Express* on Piccadilly Radio 261. It was to be broadcast every Saturday morning hosted by presenters Becky Want and an eighteen-year-old Chris Evans.[7] Working in the studios, watching the

Welcome to the club

presenters, learning to record interviews with a Marantz and edit on a Studer A820 with a white chinagraph 'grease' pencil and a razor blade, reviewing the singles and meeting the stars gave me the bug for doing something music-industry related with my life.

By day, I was employed as an (unwelcomed and largely unsupervised) management trainee, based at the Cooperative Wholesale Society Travel and Banking Group, but at the weekends and by night I was moonlighting recording the club / gig reviews and random reports that I'd pitched and managed to land with Chris Whatmough and John Clayton.[8] I hated my day job, but I loved working for Piccadilly Radio 261.

Reporting for *Saturday Express* gave me a pass into one of the best clubs in the world. I called the Haçienda head office and told them that I was a journalist working on a story about nightlife for the *Manchester Evening News* and Piccadilly Radio.[9] It was a total blag but it worked. Guest list for me and five friends with free drinks? Sorted. Access to the DJ and VJ booth with interview time set aside? Sorted. Lifetime VIP membership for me? Sorted. Once my friends had drunk all the free drinks and were happy dancing I disappeared upstairs. I spent the rest of the evening watching the visuals and the dancefloor from above and bouncing between the DJ booth and the VJ booth where I chatted with the filmmaker Dani Jacobs next door. Back at Piccadilly 261, as brilliant as I thought my feature was, it was considered too grown up for *Saturday Express*, so they canned it. Their loss. My gain.

Music, clubs and entertaining people has been my happy place since my mum, Blanche, went into labour with me and my twin while she was singing onstage at the Free Trade Hall (as family legend goes). I was fifteen when I started clubbing, using my sisters' birth certificates on rotation for ID to gain membership to clubs like PiPs, DeVilles, Rotters and The Ritz. When I had my eighteenth birthday at Berlin Nightclub on Deansgate I'd already been a regular there for two years. I was always able to talk my way into anywhere and I was so keen and affable that the security waved me through without the need for payment.

Later years saw me singing in bands and recording studios as a lead and backing singer in hype spots like Out of the Blue, Spirit and Roger Boden's 'The Cottage'. I was a second lead singer for a band called Bernie Hot Hot,[10] and we performed live at the International I and II supporting Curtis Mayfield and Deacon Blue on separate occasions. A few years later I recorded backing vocals for a band called KAOS, performing showcases at Metropolis and SARM West in London.[11] I wrote my own music for a while, remaining unsigned and unpublished before returning to my academic path when I was accepted for an English Literature degree at Manchester Polytechnic in 1991.[12] Not long after that everything went wrong, and I became a DJ.

I hit the ground running with a party at the Number 1 Club on Central Street, then was given my first significant residency at a monthly party called Flesh at the mythic Fac 51, The Haçienda in Manchester. I discuss Flesh, the Haçienda years and the Haçienda renaissance with the people at the sharp end of operations: Paul Cons, Peter Hook, Luke Howard, Kath McDermott and Ang Matthews[13] in the chapters that follow. My residency at Flesh enabled me to join a boys' club which changed my life, as I rose through the ranks to play in the booths of some of the most prestigious clubs around the world.

DJ'ing made it possible for me to move to London and make a career out of working in the music industry, mentored by some of the best in the business. I introduce you to Dulcie Danger – the warmup DJ from my residency at the Zap Club[14] – and discuss the incredible years working at Mercury Records where I earned my first gold record from a mix compilation for Polygram and a second one for my work with Roni Size and Reprazent with the mighty Gilles Peterson MBE.

Caroline Prothero was the first person to book me to play at the Ministry of Sound in London. She was the first woman in the straight world whom I heard loudly banging the drum for equality in clubs and the music industry. I discuss gender politics, meeting people at their level and having big ideas with her. From 1998 to 2001 I was the Promotions and A&R Director for Azuli Records. I compare management notes and bringing a small independent into the world of major-label styled promotion with the then owner, David Piccioni.

At the turn of the millennium, I became a full-time, freelance DJ and a resident for Ministry of Sound International, touring Asia, India, South America and Europe. I also discovered that I had a love for and a growing fanbase in Paris[15] and Montreal. I've got up to all sorts, good and bad, while DJ'ing: the chapter 'Bad behaviour: shit shags and crap hotels' is a brief confessional with penance included.

Encouraged by my growing popularity, I moved to Paris in 2004. Four months later I was given a police escort through the streets of central Paris to play a historic outdoor party to 30,000 people for the Solidays organisation. For the next eight years The City of Light shone down on me. Termed by many as 'La Belle Epoque', my years as a resident at Mix Club have passed into legend. *Paulette in Paris* is a book on its own.

The years 2012–15 were when pretty much every business decision I made was wrong and I have never felt less

Introduction

welcome to the club. I felt stuck in a groove I could not jump out of. I forced quit, simultaneously resigning from Radio FG, my residency at Queen Club and my booking agent. My failure to act on the red flags already raised meant that I moved to Ibiza only to bang my head against the impenetrable white walls for two years. Making the decision to leave Ibiza was hard but life on the White Island was unsustainable for me, a single, freelance DJ. I'd flown too near the sun and fell to earth, making a soft landing in Manchester.

In the ten years since I left Paris, I have learned a lot about myself, my career and this industry. Living in Manchester has given me the space and the strength to build some bridges and begin a crusade to stake my place in the history of the culture itself. First, I reconnected with my family. Then I broke everything down to ground zero, and slowly came to know the people and the city I'd been away from for twenty-one years. I had to find regular work, my own place and people who believed in me enough to help me make something of my talents and not talk me out of them like they had in Ibiza. The bars in Manchester's Northern Quarter slowly provided this. I started small with a First Birthday Party for Nick De Sousa at Tariff and Dale. From there I was heard by bookers and owners from Albert's Schloss, Cottonopolis and a few more bars around town. It was hard graft and disagreements with bookers and bar managers over equipment, conditions and pay were many. I examine this chaotic rupture, why and how my life went from wonderland to warzone and discuss the importance of planning your career in the chapter 'How to Kill a DJ'. This chapter was hard to write and makes for uncomfortable reading.

If this book teaches anything it's how to be stubbornly resilient in the face of adversity. Outside of the hermetically sealed Ibiza bubble, I became aware that there are women like me in this industry, and that, despite blatant discrimination, we are all growing beautifully into our later-years careers. Four years prior to this I'd been led to believe that I was over. I discuss women's secret legacy and more women's rights-related issues in the chapter 'FAQs (female asked questions)', with my crack team of disruptors, goddesses, entrepreneurs and suffragettes, which include Jamz Supernova, Marcia Carr, DJ Colleen 'Cosmo' Murphy, Judy Griffith, Gladys Pizarro, and Radio 1's *Introducing Dance*'s Jaguar, Erica McKoy, NIKS, Lakuti and Naomi Pohl. We can all learn from them.

When I was little, success was marked by seeing a Black person with a regular role on the television or hearing them daily on the radio. I was riveted by the BBC's *Play Away* and *Play School*[16] programmes, not just because I loved the round and square windows and presenters in colourful dungarees, but because there was a woman who looked like me. She publicly embraced her Blackness and wore her colourfully beaded braids and extensions like a badge of ethnic honour. She was also responsible for the numeracy, literacy and social etiquette of a generation. I didn't have any Black teachers all the way through school: I wasn't taught by anybody who even vaguely represented me or my family's culture or lives, so seeing this woman on the television, at a peak hour and in a position of authority was immense.

I wanted to be Floella Benjamin (now Baroness Benjamin). Yet, as proud as I was of her as I watched her at home on TV, at school my classmates used her name as a playground taunt to poke fun at me and my twin as they ran around us in a ring. Children – and racism – in the seventies could be cruel. We were 'othered' through her, jeered at for how she looked, how she spoke and acted. We were forced to laugh at her along with them. We also knew that if we laughed at her we were laughing at ourselves by proxy. The primary-school years were fraught with the contradictions of white privilege. That this has persisted into the present day is hugely depressing.

Baroness Floella Benjamin says: '"When you are Black you carry your colour with you everywhere you go ... You're always having to face it. You saw what happened to the boys when they missed those penalties at Euro 2020, the venom that came out. So you know it's there in society."

'But she sees the positive change in society – the white people clearing up the vandalised mural of Marcus Rashford after that penalty miss, for instance. If the bowling alley incident happened now, she says, "white people would rush in to defend me"'.[17]

These hard facts, spoken by a Black, African, female septuagenarian Baroness, hit differently. The 2021 Government Commission on Race and Ethnic Disparities stating that racism is non-existent in the UK was deeply flawed. The power of fearless activism heightened political awareness, and social media meant that it was not given a pass. The report was pilloried as a travesty. In the aftermath of the Rashford mural scandal and the racist Euros reaction, speaking truth to power became a force to be reckoned with. Now angels can rush in where fools dare to tread.

Even so, the music industry is not without its issues or disadvantages. There are so few Black and female role models behind the decks or in the boardrooms, and this needs to be addressed. There is an undercurrent of racism and sexism, while stories of misconduct are only now starting to come to light. Not everyone is comfortable with outspokenness. In recent years, we have been shocked by the opposition of women minimising and dismissing the experiences of other women and non-binary people, both online and in the press. It is dispiriting how quickly the flippant, undermining comments of one person can destroy the good work and character of many (especially when they've barely read the post let alone the article), depriving others of necessary knowledge. To #breakthebias[18] we must challenge the hobby / ornament / token narrative on women DJ'ing and on women's place in the music industry. We are all serious professionals with singular experiences and styles, whose contribution is of equal importance and benefit to the industry, to the community and to the world at large. I argue for diversity, equality, recognition and full remuneration.

By 2016 the qualities that many had said would work against me were now my armour. Less afraid to show up as my unfiltered, unedited, authentic self, I sought allies who would help me to explode the stereotypes and change the narrative in the press and the university textbooks. The centenary of women's suffrage in 2018, an article in the *i* newspaper,[19] and Alison Surtees' exhibition 'Portrait of Women in Manchester Music', together with my 'Homebird' exhibition at The Lowry art gallery all encouraged the wider discussion. The battle for facts over fiction, the writer's role in fixing this and the revelation of hidden histories fundamental to accurate reporting were drawn into question. I discuss the importance of support and balanced editorial with Kamila Rymajdo.[20]

I've often felt that my travels around the world had given me sufficient material to write a book. Yet I could never understand why some people laughed at the idea when I presented it. I am a mature, articulate adult with a rich and varied work history, so why did the people around me feel I was capable of so little, worthy of so little respect, that

Introduction

I had no relevance and nothing to say? I discuss editorial bias with Carl Loben,[21] Frank Broughton, Bill Brewster,[22] Peter Hook and Dave Haslam, and suggest that a law should be passed where every book introduction should start with: 'History is never only one person's opinion and context is everything.'

For a period of ten years, electronic dance music and the associated media experienced a whitewashing that was extreme in its execution. Without realising, I was caught up in it. Black people were seen less and less behind the decks, on the magazine covers, and were almost non-existent in the editorial content or end-of-year charts for online magazines, digital stores and streaming services. We were locked out and being slowly phased out. The middle finger, DIY culture sprung from this using Soundcloud, university and pirate radio, the Internet, and social media platforms to their advantage. Some of the finest female presenters / broadcasters on air today emerged from this fertile petri dish. The initiative, commentary and rise of stars like Jamz Supernova Jaguar, Erica McKoy, Anz, NIKS and Sherelle is notable.

The pandemic and lockdown took a sledgehammer to the industry and to my mental health. The high-ranking #metoo litigation[23] and the aftershocks of George Floyd's murder turned the tension up another notch. In the chapter 'Sane as it ever was' I explore the journey through the pandemic with the people and organisations I worked with who refused to surrender in the face of this invisible assailant. The music and events industry has changed in many ways since 1991. It, and the people interviewed here, has survived the biggest head-on collision and continues to make an impact on the world. Before Queen Elizabeth II passed away, a Platinum Jubilee concert was staged outside Buckingham Palace.

Real change does not happen overnight, it takes baby steps and selfless personal acts. It stares wrongdoing in the face and challenges it, rather than excusing it as the dysfunction of failed systems or as errors that can be eliminated with a swift lexical, legislative or policy tweak. I risked my career and put my reputation on the line, but I had the courage to stand up for what I believe in. I was ready to take on the work and the world.

It has taken ten years, disillusion and disappointment and a tectonic political shift, together with the evolution of hashtag activism,[24] for me to start to fully understand and know my worth and value my achievements. My struggles with mental health, the nervous breakdowns (yes plural) that floored and changed me have added a premium. Sometimes you need to live a little, love a lot, fall in the middle, and lose the plot before opportunity knocks loud enough for you to hear it and your voice rings out loud enough for people to hear what you have to say. When Manchester University Press approached me to write this book in April 2021 I found a home with editors eager to listen, to mentor and who could get my story commissioned and into print.[25] Those were the years that shook the worst, then the words, out of me. Never give up.

If Covid, lockdown and the continuing pandemic has taught us anything it's that while we are bullet-proof survivors, the music and events industry, and every freelancer contracted to work within it, is vulnerable. From Glastonbury to the Haçienda and all the clubs, bars and events that make up the yearly calendar, this industry needs the government's support, understanding and empathy. I travel back to the lockdown years with key personnel from the Haçienda, Worldwide FM, Escape to Freight Island and the Warehouse Project to map out a survival route should this happen again.[26]

Introduction

The most beautiful bloom that has sprung from the pandemic is a renewed sense of community. The four foundation stones of acid house – Peace, Love, Unity and Respect – have become buzzwords again. We are all connected. You can put a bet on it that the person who sends you a tweet one day will be the person to save your life with a kind word or deed on another. The person who sends you records on Monday might soon be heading one of the biggest global brands, the person working in the cloakroom on Sunday could become the next resident or the biggest DJ in the world, the person stuffing envelopes could become the MD of a major record label or the Musical Director for a fashion house. And the person you exchange numbers with on the dancefloor could be running one of the top clubs in the world in ten years' time, so be good to everyone.

In the last seven years since moving back to Manchester, I've worked for and in collaboration with some spectacular talents who have and continue to contribute massively to the industry, both in front of and behind the scenes. My fierce future forces are the activists and disruptors who are making history, each pushing the agenda for radical, political and social change and applying pressure daily. This is 'Anarchy in the UK' version 2.0.2.2. They are self-confident, self-sufficient, outspoken and are not afraid of pissing a few important people off. They know themselves and don't need anyone else's validation. This is the stuff that MBEs are made of.

Welcome to the club reminds us that we are all and should all be in this together. It gives you the opportunity to absorb and reap the benefits of the know-how of some of the finest in the business – they are game-changers, all. That my life has intertwined with theirs makes me feel like the luckiest person in the world. How did I land so well?

Welcome to the club

By following my heart and my passion, by making mistakes and learning from them, by taking the advice of others yet treading my own path. I am a work in progress, as we are all, and always learning. My family and friends support network has been crucial to my survival.

But are we welcome?

Statistics don't lie, line-ups are still male dominated and female-lite and the club is still a boys' club but it is certainly less of one. Women like Annie Mac, Honey Dijon, The Blessed Madonna and Peggy Gou are now global brands and AAA-list headliners. They are doing business better than anyone before them. They have full creative control, impressive portfolios, are certainly earning better money than we used to, and they are making waves in more disciplines than their male counterparts. By the time this goes to print I will also have been given a Lifetime Achievement Award,[27] one of the key bastions of exclusivity, thus one of the warmest welcomes I could hope to receive. Long may this continue.

And do I still love it? Of course, I do. And my love grows stronger every year.

So here it is, and here I am, filled with blood and fire, sweat and tears, feeling occasionally salty but most times sweet. I'm ready to share my passion, my pain and the lessons I've learned with you, in the safe space of this book. Each situation has been recounted as accurately as possible (although some names have been changed) and the interviews and quotes have been reproduced in trust and good faith. Some people have not been included at their request, due to clashing projects and schedules. It pains me that, in this way, even I am guilty of hiding the histories of others. Finally, I hope that the knowledge of the stars within (many of them Northern) will serve as much as a beacon of light,

Introduction

inspiration and hope for you as they do for me and that they show you that even in the darkest of times with faith, this amazing community full of love, laughter, friendship and music will light your way home. I hope that you can feel the love all of us feel for the music and this culture, and that it inspires you to embark on your own journey.

Thank you for joining us for this ride. And welcome to the best club in the world.

1
Finders keepers: in the beginning

I've seen New Year's Eve in numerous locations around the world. I've headlined parties many times in Paris but found that France is not that bothered. Ibiza has a well-deserved day of rest in advance of all things DC-10 on New Year's Day. And Manchester? This year – NYE 2021 into NYD 2022 – I am headlining the New Year's Eve party at The Refuge in the Kimpton Clock Tower Hotel.[1] It has been a journey getting here after testing positive for Covid before Christmas. A ten-day quarantine followed by reporting two consecutive days' negative lateral flow tests (LFT) sealed the deal on 30 December. And now, I am behind the decks underneath the opulent, tiled arches of the Public Bar area, regaling an exuberant crowd with a set of uplifting party disco/house.

The moment approached: 10, 9, 8, 7, 6 … As my female countdown to the New Year commenced, I realised that this year – 2022 – I have been DJ'ing professionally for exactly thirty years. Without making a fuss about the anniversary, it's the longest I have ever stuck at any job. My intimate relationships have never made it past seven years, while no other post or project has lasted longer than one good promotion or five action-packed years. The longest I have lived in any one place outside of Manchester is ten years and that was in London. So here I am, thirty years on, firing the New Year countdown through the right hand CDJ.[2] A unanimous 'Happy New Year' pierced the air, punctuated with exploding balloons. There was no 'Auld Lang Syne' but throughout the Public Bar, people were cautiously shaking hands, bumping elbows or confidently negative-LFT hugging. A few braved the dancefloor divide to bump elbows with me and wish me a Happy New Year. Sylvester's 'You Make Me Feel (Mighty Real)' (Soulwax's For Despacio remix), was cued as the first track while I enjoyed listening to the crowd screaming as they took selfies of themselves and their groups with me in their background. Meanwhile, inside my head, I was watching my career flash before my eyes, amazed at how I got here and thrilled by the promise of what's still to come.

And those flashbacks?

Being a naive, twenty-four-year-old, unhappily married wife in suburban Stockport and a mature Manchester Polytechnic BA (Hons) English Literature undergraduate had a certain pathos. I was young and knew nothing about life but was officially old before my time. My passion for the English language had taken precedence over my first love of music, dancing and clubbing, which was lying dormant, waiting for release. One evening, my husband encouraged me to go out, chaperoned by our friend Tommy (who had recently come out). We went to the Number 1 Club[3] because Tommy said that women were safe there, and with my shaved head I would have no trouble fitting in.

I'd channelled Faye Dunaway in *Bonnie and Clyde* for my outfit, co-ordinating a white hooded cotton blouse and an outsize French Connection black blazer with maxi culottes, flat patent leather boots and a gaucho hat. The club was quiet; a few people were midweek drinking at the bar and less were on the dancefloor. As the DJ played the Junior Vasquez remix of Prince's 'Gett Off', I was jump-started into life. I danced on every available inch of the dance floor as the song opened a portal that had been welded shut by my marriage. When the record stopped, the manager, Paul, offered me a job go-go dancing on Friday and Saturday for £50 a night. I accepted. Taking a job to do something I loved, that came naturally and to get paid for it was a no-brainer. Only, once you take certain things out of the box, they never go back in in the same way.

My husband agreed that my go-go dancing would help to pay the bills and pay towards my studies, but he had a problem with how it looked. The women on my street had day jobs and those who didn't were stay-at-home mothers. They did not go to university, nor did they work nights dancing scantily clad in a nightclub. The nightshift workers we knew worked in transport, print, post offices, factories, or hospitals. Nineties' gender stereotyping laced with small-mindedness and suspicion made home life unpleasant. I still did it. I was good and built a profile, becoming a 'face' on the clubbing / gay scene.

Soon after, Tommy introduced me to a woman called Adele, who was launching a night at the Number 1 Club. She had exhausted her budget on club hire and flyers and couldn't afford a name DJ for the night. Tommy had told her that I had lots of records so we met, talked about music and she must have been desperate because she offered me (who had never DJ'ed anywhere before) the gig. I was booked to play from 9 p.m. to 2 a.m. for the princely sum of £30. I had no turntables, no training and no one to ask for help but it seemed like a great idea, so I agreed. I was offered one practice session at Adele's friend's house but he was so precious about his decks that he only let me touch them for long enough to put two records on and blend one into the other. He was convinced that I would break them by just looking at them.

The week of the gig I spent my entire grant for that term – £150 – on records and on the night, I packed as much vinyl as I could into two milk crates and one 7" vinyl carry box. The SUS laws and the negative attitude to gay culture and clubs in the city centre meant that I was more anxious about getting stopped by the police on the late-night drive back home than I was about DJ'ing for five hours in front of people I'd never met. I wasn't worried that I had no idea what I was doing and had had no training. I hid my skimpy outfit underneath my ankle-length, aubergine Driza Bone duster coat and parked my car directly outside the club to avoid walking past Bootle Street police station. Happily, the evening and the drive home passed in a sober blur.

I can't remember my set, but I do remember not moving from the booth. I continually pestered the sound and lights tech, Ian Bushell, asking how to work the mixing desk. I did not take a toilet break. I took to it naturally, playing a selection of funk, soul, hip hop, disco and house music for five continuous hours. Everyone danced and nobody left. After the party, word of our success and my sound filtered back to Paul Cons and Lucy Scher at A Bit Ginger Productions.[4]

Despite the Haçienda being a creative melting pot of everyone and everything good in Manchester, the club had been closed in 1990 (the same year as the Strangeways Prison riots) due to extreme gang violence. Manchester had become a dour place. We had an anti-LGBT commissioner of police, James Anderton; it was the early days of equal opportunities and LGBT departments within the City Council, clubs in the gay village were generally segregated, and the straight club circuit offered a mix of spit

Welcome to the club

and sawdust pubs or 'Yuppie' wine bars, chrome, carpets and mirrors: places for celebrities and white people to play in. Black clubbers were less welcomed in the city centre and went to The Gallery, The Reno, The Ardri, The PSV, Berlin or Legends. Mixing anything other than a drink was not encouraged.

As open-minded as the Haçienda was, it did not have a gay night for its first nine years. Peter Hook says, without hesitation:

> It was mainly down to Paul Cons[5] ... Paul Cons was part of the Haçienda team; he was very well regarded and he came up with the idea for the gay night. The thing is – the normal nights shall we say – were becoming troublesome and I think Paul Cons was sensing that we needed a change in audience just for a respite.

'Flesh' represented a phenomenal shift in the concept of clubbing and brought about the most striking pivot for the Haçienda and Manchester, flooding it with an out and proud, mixed, diverse, cash rich and up-for-it midweek clientele.

> The interesting thing for me, was that Rob Gretton, Paul Mason and Paul Cons had been trying for years to get a late license. Nobody was granted a late license in Manchester for any reason, so everything always finished at 2 a.m. That used to cause a lot of problems. So, Paul Cons tried to get a late license for this new night and lo and behold he was the first promoter in Manchester to get one. Now, I don't know if you know how you get a licence, but it has to be passed by a committee of seven people. And the reason that Flesh got it was because five of the committee were gay ... I don't know if those five guys from the licensing committee were coming down to Flesh [laughs] – we live in hope – but it was an interesting turn of events. Flesh was the first night to get a late license and it revolutionised Manchester in that respect. And what happened then, what was interesting was that the

Flesh Nights were wild in a really nice way, in the same way in which the '86–87 nights were wild and great.

But look how that backfired. Once the gangsters heard how wild it was, they all came down and had a night off. Got up to all sorts on an evening when they could. They were trying to get in because they could relax in the same way that my wife used to be able to go ... because she could relax – they don't get harassed. And that was the reason the Haçienda was open – they needed a safe place for everyone. And the sad thing from '90 to '91 onwards on the other nights it wasn't safe for anyone. Yet Flesh was different.

The idea for Flesh was inspired by the places Paul Cons had been clubbing in London and New York. He was heavily influenced by what he'd seen there and wanted to do something similar in Manchester. Paul remembers:

In the eighties Tony Wilson used to pay for me to go to New York for creative inspiration [he laughs]. Flights were about £300. I went with my best friend, the Haçienda videographer, Dani Jacobs, and we stayed in the seedy Washington Square Hotel ... it was my equivalent of when Danny Rampling went to Ibiza. I had my first E-trip at The Paradise Garage on a Saturday night. It was the full religious experience: my mind got totally blown; Black gay club, music and the whole atmosphere. I came back and thought – we've got to do this. I knew what was going to happen – I'd already seen how ecstasy could influence the clubbers.

I also went to The Love Machine at The Tunnel, The Palladium – just caught the tail end of the New York clubbing moment. Aids had started to impact the whole thing so it didn't last much longer.

In August 1991 Lucy Scher put on the Lesbian Summer of Love at The Academy. I was always nervous – I'd tried to do this in 1985 with 'Gay Monday'. I had forty people rattling around to The Communards, Joan Collins Fan Club (Julian Clary) hi-nrg and disco and punk but it didn't cross over. I was worried about getting enough people to fill the Haçienda but when Lucy did Summer of Love and got 1,000 lesbians – it was clear that we were in business, but we needed to make it more than just a gay male thing. If we opened it out to a more diverse audience – lesbians and gays – and to a more diverse audience, then we'd get the numbers ...

We were pushing through and there were a lot of people who were hostile. Everyone was ready to have a party because of Aids, the fear was intense. The one thing Covid didn't do was pinpoint a people or a culture for being the cause of the disease. Worse than that was the internalised, toxic self-hatred the government campaign and public treatment of it created. The fundamental core of gay people is having same sex. That is always in the background. Coming to terms with the reaction to that fuelled Flesh. We wanted to make a statement about gay culture – 'We are out, we are here and we are going to reclaim what it is to be gay' – that was the whole queer thing. Not to be on the defensive, to embrace it and celebrate it.

The permitted age for entering any club in Manchester at that time was eighteen. The age of consent for same sex relations in 1991 was twenty-one. Flesh was openly encouraging breaking the law.

*

A few weeks after the Number 1 party, Adele and I met with Paul Cons and Lucy Scher. The music for the main room was mainly house and we knew that they were looking for an alternative sound and feel for the second room. My husband was less happy about this. I saw DJs and DJ'ing as the evolution of performance: an equivalent and future replacement for singers or bands. It was performance that I had control of. My husband saw DJ'ing as a temporary hobby that earned decent money but would soon burn out. He couldn't have been more wrong.

Flesh launched with eye-popping neon blue, pink and yellow type-led visuals that have become synonymous with

Ben Kelly's architecture and black and yellow chevrons in the club and as iconic as Warhol's soup cans. Paul says:

> Part of it was a reaction to how house had become dark and unglamorous and to bring that sexiness back was part of it. There's been a long Haçienda tradition of doing more design-led promo. I loved the whole Andy Warhol New York seventies vibe and that's very much the style that Trevor and Craig Johnson[6] delivered for our event.
>
> I can remember the opening night at Flesh like it was yesterday. I can remember basically being stood in the club and looking at all the people and thinking, 'Wow, I can't believe that we've actually pulled this off and that we've got this crowd, this queer gay lesbian crowd in Manchester. I'd had a dream of doing that since I'd got involved in the Haçienda in 1984 … The smoke machine, nudity, the colour of it all, the glamour, all of that sticks with me.

The thing that sticks with me the most is the monthly riot in a sweatbox in front of and behind the makeshift DJ booth that they'd set up in the corner of The Gay Traitor. It was guerrilla. The turntables were housed in a massive metal flight case and balanced on two wobbly circular bar tables with a large, unsecured and unsafe, freestanding speaker to each side. Adele and I were in full view from the mezzanine. People danced on the seating behind me, on the bars, swung from the rafters and danced on the stairs. The vinyl in my record box and milk crates was constantly sent skidding across the wet, gritty floor. Someone always kicked the plug out from the wall socket or tripped over the extension lead as it was never taped down and this frequently stopped the music. The space was heaving with sweaty, tops-off bodies and it got so steamy that the speakers and amp repeatedly cut out. The fact that Adele didn't have any records or headphones of her own and never put a record on unless Paul or Lucy passed through the room never fazed us. We'd have been idiots to turn down DJ'ing as a duo at the Haçienda on this minor technicality.

I soundtracked the Pussy Parlour[7] with a playlist of extensively classic Black soul music, disco divas and funked up psychedelia: strong vocals, funky beats and classic songwriting that makes people dance and sing along. Adele and I faked our double act for a few months, but we were exposed when I had to walk in the fashion show on the main floor. Adele hosted the Pussy Parlour alone without headphones, without the music that people had come to expect in that room, without the connection to the crowd that it took to power the dancefloor. It was a disaster that nearly ended my career, and which got her fired. It was then they found out she had been collecting half the fee for doing nothing. I begged Paul and Lucy to give me another chance, and they put me on three months' probation to host the room alone.

With its clandestine mezzanine booths, young, sexy, fashionable, knowledgeable, raucous and unforgiving crowd, the Pussy Parlour became a popular addition to Flesh. Learning how to DJ in real time in front of a real crowd, figuring out how best to curate the soundtrack for the party without having the equipment at home to practise on was madness and I loved it. If I made a mistake or if I played a record that the crowd didn't like, the Sheffield crew, namely Robert Shaw (play 'Rock Creek Park' or 'Make It Happen'), Paul Murashe, Little Anthony Watts and Renaldo would give me the baseball T 'time out' hand signal until I changed the record. I put such a stamp on that room that Paul Cons only allowed me to guest upstairs for the main floor once. He said that no one else could replicate the atmosphere needed downstairs. Creating that kind of high-octane energy has become a trademark of mine.

Finders keepers

One of Paul Cons's principal influences for Flesh was Queer Nation in London – a predominantly Black gay space that had opened the year before. Paul Cons and Patrick Lilley (the Queer Nation promoter) were more friends than competitors. In his words, they were 'like co-conspirators'. I asked Patrick Lilley about Queer Nation and he simply said 'Queer Nation was Luke Howard'. Hosting the Pussy Parlour introduced me to Queer Nation and the 'Kinky Gerlinky' family as – once Adele was fired – I had the pleasure of playing alongside Princess Julia, Jeffrey Hinton, Rachel Auburn and Luke Howard.

Of our first meeting, Luke says: 'I can always remember the first time I saw you. I was just like transfixed and I said to Paul and Lucy "who's that?" and they said "that's our new DJ, Paulette". I was so glad that you were there at Flesh and giving out that energy.'

Queer Nation was Luke's first proper residency – it was where he learned how to DJ. He reminisces, 'Princess Julia was obsessed with music too and was super upfront and she was really good at getting new stuff. It was a lovely crowd, very Black, gay and mixed crowd. They were really into the music. We started it in 1990.'

In 1991 he flew to New York where he went to The Shelter and The Sound Factory. Luke says:

> David Piccioni[8] told me about The Shelter. He said, '... it's where all the old garage heads are going and it's the closest thing to The Garage [Paradise] that you're going to get.' When I went, Timmy Regisford blew my mind. I was not taking drugs and there was no booze there and I'd never heard a lot of those records played on a really good system. Hearing it sonically – only four years after The Garage had shut – watching the energy in the room and it blew me away. He was playing vinyl and I'd never heard anyone mix like that to disco records. The original Shelter was a special party.

Welcome to the club

And I remember talking to people afterwards outside on the street and they were still mourning that The Garage wasn't open any more. I can remember him playing (Harold Melvin and the Bluenotes) 'The Love I Lost' and you really felt that record. It was '91, people were dying of Aids, things had changed, The Garage was no longer there, you just felt that record, everyone was singing it. I got goosebumps. You really got the sense of how much and for how long it had meant something for those people – the need to be there, to listen, to dance together – it was so strong still.

I went to New York and San Fran – I came back with so much energy hearing that music and seeing those people and that helped me with what I wanted to do with Queer Nation and what I wanted to play. It was like a real inspiration.

It's a bit like, you know when the old acid house / Balearic DJs talk about going to Ibiza, having that moment. For me those nights out at Shelter and on the gay scene – nowhere was playing that music. It [the nineties London gay scene] was really hard and really white, whereas Queer Nation – it was a sort of 'High on Hope' gay version. Or Zoo and Paul Trouble Anderson – our little gay version of that. We had so many great PA's – Barbara Tucker, Juliet Roberts and Patrick Lilley used to get guest DJs from the Ministry of Sound, which opened in '90–'91. Sometimes the agents would ask Patrick, 'Do you want to have Frankie on the Sunday'. So we had François Kervorkian, Frankie Knuckles, Louie Vega, Tedd Patterson. Capacity 250 – Bank Holiday we opened up through to Rock Garden – Michael Watford, Ultra Nate, Joi Cardwell and a crowd that were really into the music and dancing.

Flesh relied on the strength of its residents and never got into booking big American DJs for the night, but it regularly featured performances from artists like Leigh Bowery, Divine David (artist David Hoyle), Adeva, Juliet Roberts, M-People, Pet Shop Boys, Take That, and featured risqué fashion shows from fetish designers Murray and Vern, or glamourous choreographed happenings from the likes of Vivienne Westwood, Destroy and Pam Hogg.

There were no schools, academies, degree, HND or BTEC courses, there were no mentors or internships available where I could learn about my blossoming DJ career. I had no friends with DJ equipment, it wasn't a common (or a cheap) hobby. In the nineties you were considered weird or special if you took art as an option. DJ'ing was nowhere near the curriculum and any self-help books hadn't been written yet. Without support, equipment or direction, I figured out how to make my sets better and found ways to make myself visible to the world. I applied to all the London record labels to be on their mailing lists and was refused by most. To the ones that accepted me, I returned my feedback / reaction sheets and charts. I made occasional phone calls (landline) or sent messages by fax or letter.[9] Gordon Knott at *DJ Magazine* started publishing my Top 10 charts regularly.[10] That put me on the radar of clubs and promoters outside of Manchester.

I started investing in building my record collection and improving my set. I always packed a healthy selection of records to cover every mood. I learned how to read a room, feel the crowd and played a different set every night. I never planned a set by writing lists or playlists and I knew nothing about beats per minute (BPMs). No one taught or coached me; the years I spent clubbing gave me an instinct for the songs and the reaction I would need at different times of the night.

Women were unarguably a special ingredient in the Flesh recipe. Lucy made a point of putting women upfront, crediting us equally on posters, flyers and line-ups. When I asked Paul about this he said:

Lucy was the major influence ... she had used female DJs at the Lesbian Summer of Love and wanted to continue and also we felt it would fit well with the lesbian and gay vibe we were going for. I think the main benefit was broadening the diversity of the event, attracting a bigger, different audience, plus of course their music was brilliant. Lucy brought that: a strong woman at the centre of the whole operation meant that the other people she brought in gave it this whole other element. When Lucy did it, it had that diversity, which was not really something that some of the other clubs like Trade pulled off.

In April 1992, Kath McDermott joined the team. She muses: 'It never even crossed my mind to be a DJ – it wasn't a thing then … I didn't have a clue what was going on really, but I definitely knew how to party. And I knew about dancefloors because I was one of those people. I just loved clubbing.'

Apart from being one of Lucy's neighbours in Hulme, Kath and her partner Lin had created their own monthly event in Liverpool called 'Loose'.[11] Kath had also previously played for Paul and Lucy at Queer Academy alongside Tim Lennox, and when Lucy and Paul started to set up Flesh, they went over to see Kath play at Loose in Liverpool. They loved the energy of the party and the crowd they had created and wanted Kath and Lin to bring this crowd to their event in Manchester.

As the Loose DJs, Kath and Lin were chosen to play on the main floor as residents on rotation alongside the mighty Tim Lennox and the maverick Dave Kendrick. Of this time Kath says: 'I was doing my final year then and graduated in 1992, so it was all going on then.'

While there were other visiting female guests for the occasional Saturday night and Haçienda birthday parties,[12] Kath and I are the only two women to have held down a regular monthly residency at the Haçienda.

There were no online or streaming services like Beatport, Traxsource, iTunes or Spotify, so regular trips to record shops, markets and second-hand shops were routine. Friends, Simon Bushell, Andy Moore and Steve Machin, created a vinyl distribution company in Manchester called NorthSouth, which was linked to Simply Red's management company, So What: from there I sourced pre-release white labels like Robin S's 'Show Me Love' and Gabrielle's 'Dreams', and bought advanced, imported and reissued vinyl. I bought imports from Eastern Bloc, Spin Inn and Manchester Underground Records,[13] back catalogue tunes from Vinyl Exchange, Piccadilly Records, the record stalls in the Corn Exchange and Fennel Street, then there was Affleck's Palace and lunchtime shopping sessions in Stockport.

I fought for recognition as a serious DJ among the DJ staff of the elite underground record shops. One Saturday afternoon, while shopping for imports in Eastern Bloc, Simon Bushell asked the guys behind the counter to include me when they were setting the special promo bags aside for the big DJs like Graeme Park, Dave Haslam, Tim Lennox, Jon Dasilva. One server argued that he didn't think I deserved it because I wasn't a serious DJ and the only reason I was getting any work at all was because I DJ'ed in fluffy bras and sequinned knickers. While it was true that I did wear those items and variations on that theme, he was missing the point. I was a weekly regular in their shop. I developed a sharper, less revealing look when I was DJ'ing in the straight clubs to prove that I could cross the boundaries and that I was a DJ for the music and not just for the show. Like DJ'ing, record shops were an exclusive boys' club – very few women worked in them and the ones who did and the ones who shopped there had to rise above the intimidating culture and competition to be taken seriously. Thankfully things – and that outmoded under-the-counter pecking order – have changed for the better.

Flesh ran for five years and Paul Cons and Lucy Scher's A Bit Ginger Productions became an incredible force for

LGBTQ+ culture, arts and Manchester clubbing. Of this Paul says:

> Even at the Haçienda there was a bit of push back, raised eyebrows. After the success of Flesh when the club was struggling, I suggested turning the Haçienda into a gay club and to make the Saturdays a big gay night – but then Paradise Factory opened and did that ... Flesh is a great example of a diverse club, and what's it given to the world? A unique moment in time that released that incredible potential. Our banner on the opening night was 'It's Queer Up North'. Flesh inspired the screenwriter Russell T. Davies and so many more. We lit the match ...

Before her death in 2018, when I thanked Lucy for giving me the chance to carve out a career as a DJ, she wrote:

> 11 June 2018
> but you
> made us shine! Happy days.
> And so glad they continue. I
> feel very proud of Flesh. It
> marked the end of the
> separatist clubs and let
> everyone party together and
> now look at the world!!!! Or the
> UK at least ...

The more I worked late and returned early, sleeping in separate bedrooms – at my husband's request – made sense. He had an early start for his job at the university, so it seemed logical, even though we'd barely been married a year. This rupture in intimacy did not stop me from trying to stay close by including and inviting him to enjoy and experience my family and my brave new world, neither of which he wanted to engage with. In the growing isolation I hoped that I could inspire in him the same level of interest and support that I gave to him with his family and life, but I was wrong.

Finders keepers

He turned up late to Flesh wearing a dishevelled, paint and plaster-splattered sweatshirt with half-mast trousers that had shrunk in the dryer and his dirty black work boots. I came off stage wearing a skin-tight, white pearlised Murray and Vern rubber all in one, with a lace-up corset and towering Vivienne Westwood black platform shoes. We couldn't have looked like more separate entities if we'd tried. The young, handsome University Lecturer / Sound Engineer I had been so excited to present to my curious bosses made zero effort to impress. Standing stony faced, arms folded, with his back pressed firmly against the pillar, he made no attempt to communicate with anyone, complaining that the music was too loud and hurt his ears. When I introduced him to Paul and Lucy, they said it was a shame that he had missed their star walking in the fashion show. In reply, he was rude and unenthusiastic about nightclubs, telling them that he detested parties. I was stunned. Was this a joke or a protest? It was an awkward, humiliating meeting that lasted seconds but felt like hours. I was nothing to him. This was nothing to him. Embarrassed by his behaviour I made excuses to Paul and Lucy, 'He's not usually like this ... he's tired ... been working odd shifts'. But in that moment I realised that he was always like that. He was always ready with the acid comments, the micro-aggressions, the politically incorrect, passive aggressive jokes, the put-downs. When he signalled to leave, I was in full flow, DJ'ing, smiling and soaking up the atmosphere. I didn't walk him to the door. Inside I was fuming and wanted to punch him, not kiss him goodbye. Our marriage freewheeled downhill hitting every obstacle in its way after that.

I had segued seamlessly from a back-up singing/songwriting housewife to an independent student and a Haçienda resident DJ who hosted the Pussy Parlour every month, downstairs in The Gay Traitor at Flesh. Two months before the Flesh first birthday party I moved out of my marital home for a trial separation that proved itself to be successful and final. I started seeing someone else and within weeks my husband had moved another woman into his bed and our house. He sent her to deliver a box of crockery and kitchenware to me, at my mother's, which shook me like a seizure. 'Oh thanks ... err ... Nice to meet you', I mumbled. Thank God for Prozac. After weeks of couples' counselling and Wythenshawe Psychiatric appointments (for me) we started the year separation that would allow us to divorce by mutual consent (plus a further three years of separation). I was sailing through the second year of my degree course but drowning in the first year of my divorce. Through this experience I learned to swim through choppy emotional waters and the good news is that it got better. Paul and Lucy offered me a Saturday night weekly residency at 'The Glory Hole' at Bar Kay,[14] playing alongside Matt Ryan and Kath McDermott. I was running a weekly Tuesday night party called Glam at the Number 1 Club. Then Paul and Lucy offered me my own room for their Saturday night party called 'The World' when they moved to HOME on Ducie Street.

My residency at Flesh at the Haçienda was unarguably the catalyst for my career. Every offer of work that followed flowed from there. Yet Manchester clubbing wasn't just about the Haçienda. There was also a vibrant DIY scene bubbling ferociously underground, which was inhabited by a cluster of Black music promoters, diverse creative directors and DJs, and once I started gigging weekly I began to work with them around Manchester.

The nineties were not an easy time for anyone Black, and more specifically Black men in the centre of Manchester.

Politically and socially there were seriously restrictive issues which meant that Black music clubs and parties were pushed to the outskirts unless they were run by white people. PACE (the Police and Criminal Evidence Act of 1984) had replaced and then expanded the SUS laws, and racial profiling was in full play in the Manchester streets at night time. Moving from Bristol to Manchester to stretch his wings, Michael Barnes-Wynter[15] is a Black Graphic Designer / Graphic Artist who was responsible for the club night called 'Hoochie Coochie' which was held at Dry Bar 201 (Fac 201) and held as a Saturday afterhours breakfast club at Oscars on Fountain Street. I was a regular fixture. He also put on fashion and art shows in and around Manchester.

He recalls that Black people weren't invited into the city centre – any city centre – in England and that the early nineties was not a 'Black creative' friendly space. Despite this, he 'has such a soft spot for Leroy Richardson',[16] who took him under his wing. Michael says:

> In 1991 I approached him to put a fashion show in Dry Bar 201. I told him that they needed decks – which they didn't have at the time. But he brought them in from the Haçienda and placed them behind the bar in the top corner where they stayed for years. The fashion show showcased local designer Ono Eno[17] and we used the bar as the runway.

Jeff Bibby's (Bubbles) Oscars was chosen as the location for the launch event and location for Hoochie Coochie in 1992. It showcased the talents of male and female DJs without discrimination and regularly showcased the talents of myself, Paula and Tabs.

> I'm a collector of souls. I found it really easy to do. I think it stems from my dad, that DJ Derrick, Star & Garter environment,[18] and being so proud of my Jamaican heritage. [I] gravitated to finding 'Who looks like me who's doing

something similar: the closest initially was Lemn Sissay – he's a poet – then there was the Jam MCs – Chris Jam and Tomlyn – they were the closest to doing things that made sense to me. There was Wayne Simmonds who was a videomaker but at the time these were all men and also the difference for me – a very SMALL group of Black men where every other party had white organisers. Black people doing something successful was rare.

Anyone in the arts or clubbing world in Manchester in the nineties can testify that Barney mixed every visual fashion code and he stood out a mile. Everyone knew who Barney was. Michael says:

I think I got away with it because I've got my own thing. I had blondish hair, wore Seditionaries suits. I liked wearing my kilts. Lemn always used to say to me how come you walk around this city with your head held high? … It appears to me that as Black creatives we had to be loud, we had to make the invisible visible, then invincible.

The Haçienda was created as a creative home for misfits. That space provided shelter and inspiration for me, Barney, Leroy, Hewan, The Jazz Defectors and Rowetta. It also made a space for a 6-foot-4 British-Jamaican Black kid from Bolton called Elton Jackson who defines himself as that 'little kid from Bristol who went to Manchester then ended up on Top of the Pops'. Elton ran a club pre-Flesh that gained enormous press notoriety, called 'Most Excellent', booking new DJs like Andrew Weatherall, Mark Moore and Justin Robertson. Paul wanted to add this decadence to the hedonistic mix, so employed Elton to take charge of the guestlist and the admissions at Flesh.

Manchester life in the nineties was a challenge. Elton says,

Someone set fire to my hair on the bus. If you were different you were running a risk … People said to me, 'How come you never got beaten up?' Boy George or Pete Burns said, 'If you go out dressed like us you have to be a runner or a fighter.' And I think I was a bit of both. But by the time I had become infamous I think the music scene had started to flourish and it became more than people just dancing in a club, it became a movement, so I began to get respect ... By the time Flesh came along, it was an amazingly brave move. I did the door for the first six months. It was important that you got the right people in the club and kept the wrong people out. It was really hard work and I think through that you meet so many people, and if you get on the door opens. You're the person on the door who knows everybody and can see in an instant whether it's a yes or no.

'91–94 we're getting / encouraging the tribes to mix, blending codes, changing the culture. The culture was very segregated. There's so much hype particularly about the Haçienda and dance music full stop. For us that were in it, we know it was brilliant because we were in it, but it wasn't safe, it wasn't mixed, and it wasn't the only place or thing. If history is to be correct, we have to acknowledge the other stories that have been squashed down and pushed out. That's how important these clubs are, and this music is because it does change people's minds.

Changing minds and challenging attitudes was the calling card of every woman of colour who stood proud behind the decks of some of the most iconic parties in the UK. We women were DJs first – known for the music we played and the style we played it with. The look was strong but also secondary. I worked an androgynous persona and exuded a fierce attitude that stood out from the smiley culture, flowing locks and baggy rave style. My shaved head started in 1989, continued as a university economy, then was finetuned after attending the Vidal Sassoon student night for a free haircut. Nick Arrojo and Peter Gray both perfected my rough space-age-meets-tribal look. My singular style (in Manchester terms anyway) soon transported me to a world of catwalk modelling and fashion shoots for local designers like Gio Goi and Consalvo Pellecchia.

One evening at home in my mum's Fallowfield sitting room, my friend Simon Bushell presented me with an advert that he had cut out of the local newspaper. Granada TV were auditioning for presenters for a new show called *Juice*. It was a lifestyle culture magazine programme which would be in scheduling competition with Terry Christian and Dani Behr's *The Word* on Channel 4. It was aimed at the prime-time youth market with an 18–30 demographic. I applied, as did hundreds more. I was amazed when I received my letter for the recall and elated when I got the job presenting alongside Tara Newley[19] and Johnny Dangerously.

At twenty-three years old, Janie Valentine was the youngest producer with Granada TV. From 1993 to 1994 she was responsible for the team who created *Juice*. Flying in the face of the homophobia created by the Aids campaign, programmes such as this heralded the start of positive images of gay culture entering this broadcasting medium. Nowadays we have *Gentleman Jack*, *It's a Sin*, *Sex Education* and *Banana* on lock. The legislative aftershocks of Section 28 that prohibited the promotion of homosexuality by local authorities were not repealed until 2004. Prior to this, anything gay on TV was considered an advertiser's graveyard like *Soap*, terrifying (the Aids campaign), shocking (*The Naked Civil Servant*) or crass, camp and a send-up like Dick Emery in bad drag – Liverpool comedian Kenny Everett dressed as Dolly Parton with a beard or John Inman in *Are You Being Served?* Dramas such as Russell T. Davies's *Queer as Folk* and the adaptation of Armistead Maupin's *Tales of the City*, which became the must-watch cult programmes of the decade, were the exception. While a regional programme, *Juice* played its part in this explosion of queer culture, running features on Flesh, Manchester's drag scene, the launch of Paradise Factory, and comedy from Lily Savage[20] just after the watershed. It was fun, sexy, irreverent and anarchic. It featured a clubby soundtrack with lots of house music and live appearances, and put *me*, a bald, Black, queer, female presenter on primetime TV every Friday night at 9 p.m. Ground-breaking.

*

My activism snapped into focus when I signed up to present *Loud and Proud* alongside Boy George and *The Word*'s Hufty. It was the first gay magazine programme to be broadcast on national radio. Produced by Mark Ovenden and Christopher Kelly for Fergus Dudley at Radio 1, *Loud and Proud* took a weekly topical look at LGBT issues. It was not an easy launch – the heads at the BBC were unsupportive and the press had a field day – but I wasn't fazed. The show was relevant, necessary and I am proud to have been a part of it.

In less than two years I had become a local celebrity with features in *i-D*, *The Face*, *Mixmag* and *DJ Magazine* and lead articles in the *Manchester Evening News* and *City Life*. I was becoming a nationally recognised DJ. I was co-presenting a radio show on BBC Radio 1, I was being namechecked in liner notes for Kinky Trax house-music compilations and was presenting a popular TV programme on Granada TV. I'd had a speaking part in the first episode of *Cracker* alongside Robbie Coltrane which gave me my 'fast track' Equity Card. I presented the Manchester Festival programme alongside Anthony H. Wilson at prime time on Granada TV. I bought my first set of Technics turntables, a mixer, amp, tape decks and speakers from Andy Aindow at

Welcome to the club

The Bassment DJ Supplies with my first pay cheque from *Juice*. I also engaged an accountant, submitting my first tax return as a self-employed freelancer and DJ. I'd achieved all this by the time I graduated in 1994.

As I completed my finals, Wayne Kurz booked me at the Zap Club in Brighton[21] as a guest. The party was so successful that he asked me to take up a weekly Saturday-night residency. At the same time, I was invited to be a regular guest at REACT's Garage night at Heaven[22] and my DJ diary was filling up with dates across the UK. With my divorce now imminent, the job that I never applied for became the career that I pursued. I followed my passion and the path less travelled to become a full-time DJ.

2

London to Paris: Eurostar

If there was ever a crystal-ball moment, then eating hash cakes as I took a night-time taxi tour through the rainy streets of Paris and getting starry eyed with my friend Sam would be it. Sam and I had escaped from the 1997 Mercury Records Christmas do with our French Franc-filled expenses envelopes – we wanted to see the city, not sit in a bar drinking cocktails. Our tour ended with us taking two memorable shots – one of me in my Big Bird yellow puffer coat standing in front of the Louvre Pyramid. The other was of the illuminated Eiffel Tower with its countdown to the Millennium twinkling against the night sky. Paris was in me and would eventually become me, but before I could think about that, I had to move from Manchester.

When I accepted my residency at the Zap Club I hadn't considered the logistics of travelling from Manchester to Brighton, and that soon became important. In 1994 there were no high-speed trains: the journey took around six hours without counting the transfers needed from home to station, from station to station, from station to hotel and back. It was exhausting lugging two twenty-three kilo record boxes and luggage alone. I didn't have a car, so to avoid breaking my back or my shoulders, I broke the journey by sofa surfing and staying with friends in London. This wasn't ideal either so, doing things backwards, I decided to look for a place of my own after finding the club I called home.

It Girl was the party where you were blessed with a nineteen-year-old music encyclopaedia, known locally as Dulcie Danger, as my warmup / wing woman.[1] Dulcie recalls: 'When you came – it was really exciting. You came in and you had a friend with you, and you were really nice. We ended up doing a back-to-back and it was wonderful.' Thus began a mutual DJ appreciation and friendship. For nearly three years my residency[2] was a sold-out ticket but the culture at the Zap eventually became very male dominated. Club politics aside, it was a special party and fans still contact me about records I played or mixes and transitions that they only heard me play there.[3]

While I played tracks and remixes from The Young Disciples, Galliano and Incognito in my DJ sets, I never dreamed that I would work for the label or with the legendary Gilles Peterson or Norman Jay MBE (two of my DJ heroes). Call it a lucky coincidence, my next job found me my best London friend, a beautiful Black Grenadian called Wendy Douglas, who was a radio presenter on Kiss FM's *The Word*.[4] Through her I met the station head Gordon Mac and DJs Judge Jules,[5] Danny Rampling, Bobbi and Steve and Paul 'Trouble' Anderson. I'd meet Wendy at the Kiss Holloway Road studios after work on Friday. We'd eat, drink copious amounts of red wine, and get ridiculously stoned at her apartment in Hampstead Heath. We partied hard.

You could find us wherever Gilles Peterson played. Gilles played an eclectic blend of jazz, funk, disco, soulful and deep house, electronica and drum and bass which I thought was a sharp contrast to the Manchester rave culture I had come from. However, Gilles reminds me that he set up a pirate station that was happening before and during the acid-house transition. He also used to have a residency at the Belvedere Arms where he remembers playing Phuture's Acid Trax while the famed Michael Knott jazz danced to it on E. His crowds would go to Electric Ballroom on a Friday then Shoom on a Saturday. But I came in at 'That's How It Is' where Gilles, James Lavelle and Ben Wilcox packed out Bar Rumba every Monday night, playing their eclectic soundtrack to a discerning crowd of music aficionados and serious dancers.

I worked my way into Gilles's consciousness with my reviews for *Mixmag Update*, by dancing to his sets at Bar Rumba, Far East at The Blue Note in Hoxton, seeing him out and about at other clubs and being introduced to him, Janine Neye and Bee Sayed by Wendy. I was an outsider, an unknown Black, bi, female house-music-playing DJ from Manchester who didn't know anyone on the acid-jazz scene. It took a lot of Tuesday redeye to earn the honour of hanging out in that DJ booth. Once welcomed into the inner sanctum, it took the campaigning of Janine Neye[6] and Bee Sayed,[7] years and patience before eventually earning my spot behind the decks of That's How It Is, joining Gilles, Ben Wilcox and the hallowed boys' club of guest DJs who had played there before me.

Not having a car and never having lived outside of Manchester, I couldn't find my rhythm or my way around. It took me a week before I realised that Hyde Park was literally across the road from my flat. I came alive when I was in the club or DJ'ing at the weekend. I'd met with Simon Sadler, the Head of Music at Kiss FM who brusquely told me that I would never work in radio in London with a Northern accent. I was devastated. Radio was my happy place yet I couldn't find a way in. Weekdays saw me unravelling, I had lost my friends' network and I was homesick. Never one to admit defeat, I rode it out and found a job as a researcher with *Rapido TV*,[8] working on a magazine programme made for Channel 4 called *BaadAsss TV*.[9] Headed by presenters Ice-T and Andi Oliver and with voiceovers by Wendy Douglas, it was slated to be a youth arts programme for Black people and people of colour. Emulating *Rapido TV*, it quickly became a Eurotrash-styled satire of Black artists, music and culture, which wasn't what I'd anticipated. It was stressful being one of two people of colour in a production team of twelve that was pushing the comic / minstrel / exotic and sexualised stereotypes of Blackness, and I was glad when my contract and series one ended.

I received two important calls that changed the course of my herstory. One was from Eddie Gordon[10] and the other was from Gilles Peterson. Both asked if I was interested in a job working for Mercury Records as their Dance Music Press Officer. I thought it was a wind-up, so deleted the messages. A few days later there were two more urgent messages, demanding that I call Kas Mercer in the Press Department to interview for the post. I was to call both Eddie and Gilles for a brief on their respective office numbers.

The Mercury Records offices were based in an unassuming, seventies, brown and red brick, glass and steel building, which faced the plusher London Records / FFRR offices where Pete Tong[11] and Andy Thompson[12] worked. I was interviewed for half a day, spending time firstly with the formidable Head of Press, Kas Mercer,[13] and Dawn Bartlett.[14] I was then introduced to the senior managers[15] and spent a further hour with Gilles and Paul Martin,[16] who ran through their upcoming roster[17] with me. In the Fontana office I listened to a demo from a band called Lamb.[18] And to close, I spent an hour with Judge Jules (who I already knew) and

Eddie Gordon to discuss their plans for Manifesto Records.[19] It was an intense buzz and exciting day. When I got home, the message blinking on my answerphone was from Kas Mercer telling me that I had got the job and to call immediately. She faxed me the contract (which I quickly signed and returned). I was to start on Monday.

If I'd ever had a mentor or anyone who'd coached or helped me to understand the mechanics of the positions I filled, my life would have been ten times easier, but there I went again, out of my comfort zone, not knowing how to do something but doing it anyway.

I knew no other music industry PRs. I had no idea how magazines or newspapers worked, knew nothing about lead times or turn-around and had zero knowledge of the politics of competing titles, exclusivity or publicity campaigns but I was excited to learn. I had no photographer or make-up artist contacts and had never booked a taxi, hotel or flight on anyone's business account or through a travel agent for work. I knew a handful of journalists who were based in the *Mixmag* offices near my flat and at *DJ Magazine* in Farringdon, but I knew that that was nowhere near enough contacts to launch a national press campaign. I went out to the newsagents, bought every newspaper and magazine I could find and a massive address book, then meticulously cut out the mastheads[20] and pasted these into the book together with notes on what I thought each publication covered. I was all set.

My first assignment was a press junket for the new Oleta Adams album which was being held at Claridge's Hotel. I was handed the keys to a car I'd never driven before plus a plastic wallet containing an interview schedule with Oleta's suite and management details, a list of the names of the journalists attending, their telephone numbers and their time slots. My heart leapt through my mouth. There was no induction, no mentoring, no shadowing for a week. I was handed a pile of files and that was it. I didn't know what to do with the information, plus not having driven around London, I got stuck in a one-way loop somewhere behind Oxford Street. I arrived at Claridge's late and disoriented.

Oleta Adams[21] was Top of the Pops famous and I gushed embarrassingly about how big a fan I was. She was gracious in the face of my inexperience. I ordered tea and sandwiches for our interviewers, which arrived on a silver tray and were served, crustless and perfect looking on delicate porcelain. Engrossed in the interviews, I ate the sandwiches myself. When we wrapped, I felt satisfied that I'd done a full day's work so went straight home. Oxford Street was just minutes away from my flat off Bayswater Road and there was nothing else in my diary. I really didn't get it. This was the first of many disregards of my full-time contract. The second? Fantastic fact: I'm not the world's greatest at parallel parking. On Tuesday, I opened the side of my newly inherited Blue Renault Clio like a can of beans on an awkwardly positioned glazier's van that was hogging half of my space in the company car park. The damage was so bad my car was written off and I was upgraded to a custom metallic racing green Peugeot 205 1.9 GTi and a more easily accessible parking space.

When I started at Mercury Records, the press office consisted entirely of women. But in my DJ life I found the opposite to be true. I didn't meet any female DJs until 1995 when I met two Black women like me. The first was Smokin Jo[22] whose name I'd seen on the cover of DJ Magazine. She came to an after party once at my basement flat. Arriving with a glamorous entourage, she played on my decks briefly and then her party moved on. I was honoured. The meeting was short but sweet.

The other woman was Marcia Carr. Marcia was a column and reviews writer for *Blues and Soul, Mixmag Update* and *New Nation*. She also worked with Nicky Trax at the promotion company PhutureTrax and was a jazz dancer who I enjoyed dancing with on Wednesday nights at Paul 'Trouble' Anderson's legendary session called 'The Loft'. Marcia was my first Black female DJ friend outside of Manchester and the first woman DJ to be actively supportive of me in London.

This was a significant connection since Marcia was helping Alex Brierly around the office of a foundling online radio station which was called *UK Rumbal*.[23] The radio station focused on the very early grime sound and jungle, US hip hop and MC-ing but Marcia had had an idea for launching a house-music show. Citing Paul 'Trouble' Anderson and Greg Edwards, 'your bug-eyed refugee from across the sea', as her influences, she was inspired to contact people who were not regularly heard on national radio. She booked a lot of Americans whose faces, she says, dropped when they arrived, realising that they were not broadcasting from The Hilton.[24] Marcia worked hard to secure sessions with the DJs who were appearing at the Ministry of Sound[25] or at Paul 'Trouble' Anderson's night, The Loft. Her show gained respect and word spread.

As our friendship grew, Marcia invited me to do a live DJ mix and interview for her *Soundhouse Session* show. But let's just back this up a bit. Talking to friends about tuning in to an Internet radio station in 1995 was like asking everyone to get naked, ride a unicorn through the West End, sprinkling glitter and rainbows as they went. People immediately said, 'Yeah sure, that sounds like fun', but you knew they thought you were crazy.

With its AAA-list guests[26] *Soundhouse Session* was a brave, forward-thinking attempt to embrace new technology

Welcome to the club

and offer an alternative to the all-white, all British, all cut-glass diction presenter diet that terrestrial radio stations offered. Only a few places reflected the history or the diversity of the dance music community. Meanwhile, mobile phones and PDAs were not Internet ready or as popular as they are now, and most were purchased for commercial / business use only. We called people at home or work from a landline and left a message on their answerphone. A home computer was generally an Atari or Commodore. A Mac or a Windows-based PC running on a floppy disk or a CD was a rarity restricted to design businesses more than domestic users. Connecting to someone in the same house or on the same street was limited to shouting upstairs, walkie-talkies, Citizens' Band radios or a home telephone with an extension and a notepad on the side. No one had a laptop or a tablet. Anyone who could connect found that using the Internet was a minefield plagued by the instability of the signal which originally ran at 9.6 kbps ramping up to 33–64 kbps[27] with the introduction of 2G[28] in the late nineties. The network was prone to trojans, malware and viruses that could take down whole companies and continents in less time than it took to open the email it was attached to. Only those who have lived through and with the sluggish service of nineties dial-up Internet and 2G can know the horror. Thankfully, things ain't what they used to be.

In 2022, 4.39 billion people were estimated to use the Internet but in 1995 no one I knew had a home computer, less so a portable laptop, and tablets did not exist. I owned a cube-shaped Atari ST with a disk drive and a basic memory[29] that I wrote my university thesis and record reviews on.[30] It was a chunky, clunky piece of office furniture that I hid behind a hand-painted sarong that I'd bought on a truly forgettable holiday. Nevertheless, my lack of connectivity didn't stop me writing for an Internet magazine that I couldn't read, or mixing live on an Internet radio show that I couldn't hear: Internet was clearly the future. Marcia Carr had such a distinct idea, giving DJs a broadcasting break[31] when the terrestrial stations were less generous with their airtime. She was way ahead of the curve and should be recognised for this.

With my Northern accent and vocal-heavy DJ set I wasn't an obvious choice to slot into the heterosexual London club or radio circuit, but my agents worked hard and I played many prestigious dates around London and the UK.[32] I began to work with Nicky Harwood (Nicky Trax) at PhutureTrax Management, and with her booking agency secured my first international date in Portugal. Through this I learned that DJ'ing overseas requires a body-clock reset, an opening hours adjustment[33] and a flexible musical mindset. Industria with Paolo Def and Alice Cadoux (RIP) was a beautiful party in a stunning club which had limited edition gold Technics SL-1200 Mk 2 turntables, two enormous CO_2 cannons I'd never seen the like of before, which left debris on the vinyl, and bar staff who played percussion on the copper beer barrels as they served. It was magical. My second overseas date was DJ'ing alongside Mr Mike at Take 5 in Biel for Daniel Walther. It was a huge event that connected me to Swiss house-music DJ royalty. From here I was signed onto the F&G DJ Management roster for Italy and Slovenia.

Back in the UK, I received a call from Caroline Prothero,[34] a straight-talking Boltonian with a Nottingham Trent Poly background who had a propensity for running club nights and creating student parties with a political message featuring DJ newcomers like Sasha, Graeme Park and Allistair Whitehead.[35] Through this, a 1990 trip to Ibiza and being a flatmate / friend to Meg Matthews[36] she had developed a broad network of arts, fashion and London

Welcome to the club

music contacts, which included MTV's Davina McCall, Boy George and Graham Ball (Westworld). Fundraisers for London Lighthouse followed. All of which brought her to her job as a talent booker, artist liaison and events organiser for the acclaimed Ministry of Sound. Caroline was making waves in London and I was thrilled when she offered me my debut slot, playing in the Ministry of Sound bar.

As she booked me in, we had a long conversation about feminism and girl power. I found it inspiring that she believed that women should be equal in the industry and that she, like Lucy Scher, was making a point of putting women upfront on the posters, advertising and flyers and on the line-ups. In Caroline's own words:

> I was the leader of the Labour Party at school but as much as I hated her politics, Margaret Thatcher projected something positive. I was proud of being female and my femininity: I didn't want to be a man to get on, I just wanted us to get a crack ... I wanted to do what the men could do and at least share that opportunity with others like me ... I knew we women could do everything. Music was about bringing people together, sharing the vibe.

I had started to build a network of female supporters.

My set time at the Ministry of Sound was 4 a.m. till 6 a.m. so I booked a driver,[37] thus enabling me to play my set at the Zap from midnight until 2 a.m. then drive straight back to London to DJ in the Ministry of Sound bar. When we arrived, I was overwhelmed by the scale of it. It was enormous. Princess Julia was playing before me and all the pluggers from the record labels were bustling around behind her in the VIP area. The music was extraordinarily loud and the DJ console, suspended on chains, swung like a metronome to stop the vinyl skipping from the vibrations caused by the bass bins. Design-wise, it looked like the Haçienda but in every other way it was bigger and more carefully conceived. I wasn't playing on dodgy decks or wonky bar tables here. I had arrived.

While working full time and to full capacity at Mercury Records, Eddie Gordon commissioned me to mix the first Club Mix compilation, *Club Mix 96 X* in the Wisebuddah[38] studios. It was the first continuous dance music mix released on Polygram TV. Fascinating fact: while I helped curate the track list and was paid for this session, I am not credited anywhere on this album. Pre-production, the marketing man popped by my desk in the busy, open plan Press office, saying that they wanted to splash my name all over the sleeve. I'd never released an album before, had taken no professional advice about it and with the lack of privacy afforded me for this meeting, wasn't aware that what was being offered was beneficial. I distractedly suggested their doing something more tasteful – then took another call. The result? They didn't credit me at all, anywhere, but I received a gold disc when it sold over 100,000 copies.[39]

It wasn't just my DJ work that was getting attention. The artists on my Manifesto roster were climbing the national charts and my PR work had gathered momentum.

By the summer of 1997 my role and my expense account had gone into hyperdrive. This was a cause of much dissension with the accounts department who questioned why I was schmoozing a series of nobodies. To me these were the editors and features writers in the specialist dance magazines like Dom Phillips, Alexis Petridis, Dorian Lynskey, Carl Loben, Push, Ben Turner and Frank Tope but to the accounts departments they weren't important enough to merit the spend. My roster was almost entirely Black. I knew that without grassroots support the broadsheets[40] would only dedicate a small space to their discussion, but if we had a solid plan from the dance press everything and everyone else would follow. I argued that my favoured journalists were specialists who, given the opportunity, had the ambition, knowledge and ability to influence others across the board and cross my bands over into the mainstream. Everything was a battle.

Unless it was Michael Jackson or Whitney Houston, getting any press attention for an artist whose music wasn't white rock or white pop was extraordinarily challenging even if it was fresh, innovative or ground-breaking. Similarly, at Mercury Records if it wasn't Def Leppard, Metallica, Elton John or Shania Twain, selling millions of units, they didn't understand the music and would not justify the spend. If it was Black music, it was harder still.

Moreover, the dedicated Black press was considered lower in the pecking order of any promotional strategy and treated as a poor relation when it came to entertaining and hospitality. This annoyed me. The opinions the Black press had (whether about music or politics or anything in fact) didn't count for much to the people signing the cheques unless no other publication came on board or if they offered a cover feature or half the paper or magazine for the artist. Reeling off a list of take-ups from the Black press in the Monday morning meetings got the 'rolled eyes' response from every department apart from A&R. It was not encouraged to spend too much money schmoozing writers from tiny publications like *The Voice, The Gleaner, Blues and Soul, Hip Hop Connection* or *Straight No Chaser* – or the tiny dance sections of *NME* or *Melody Maker* without having a guaranteed cover or a huge feature lined up to justify the spend. Yet I could happily wine and dine a journalist from the *Guardian* who would never write about my artists and no one would question it.

My expenses always took ages to clear, and I constantly locked horns with management over their promotional elitism. To the people working in electronic dance music our world was everything, but to a major label our world was not that important. Justice was served when the writers I'd singled out were promoted to high-ranking positions or commissioned to write lead features for the broadsheets, glossies and dailies, and only when the artists on my roster grew in stature despite the obstacles and challenges from all sides. How I achieved anything with no entertaining budget is a testament to my powers of persuasion, my nose for a story and my resourcefulness.[41]

In the same year as the Labour Party and Tony Blair took over No. 10 Downing Street, there was a fresh optimism in the country. The general mood was patriotic, things were getting better while The Spice Girls and Britpop[42] ruled the roost. This was the atmosphere into which Talkin' Loud released a run of four seminal albums – *Nuyorican Soul*, Roni Size and Reprazent's *New Forms*, 4Hero's *Two Pages* and Terry Callier's *Timepeace*. Three years earlier, rave culture had been targeted by the Conservative government's Criminal Justice Bill.[43] Now, legal electronic music festivals were becoming a big deal, as were the artists booked to appear at them.

Starting with the *Share The Fall EP*, it was my job to devise a campaign for Roni Size and Reprazent[44] which would make their presence crucial to the dance music press and cross them over into the national press – not easy for a niche genre like drum and bass, the coverage of which up until then had been reserved for a tiny circulation of rave fanzines and reviews in specialist Black magazines like *Touch*, *Blues and Soul* and *Hip Hop Connection*. I had an uphill battle. *NME* and *Melody Maker* rarely gave noticeable space over

Welcome to the club

to Black music. I commissioned and organised an off-the-wall photo shoot with unconventional and unknown *Dazed and Confused* photographer Ralph Perou[45] which generated an iconic photo of Roni Size that communicated the music and the band perfectly to the press. Then I built the campaign and the supporters up from the singles through to the album release, then the live tour and festival appearances so that TV, radio and sales departments could use this coverage as a lever to seduce commissioners and afford them priority racking in the record shops. Memorable moments followed when they were nominated for awards and I confirmed the New Year cover in *Muzik Magazine*, *Mixmag* and *Future Music*.

There were losses though. When I took *Muzik Magazine* and *The Face* out to New York to cover the Masters at Work's *Nuyorican Soul* album, everything that could possibly go wrong went wrong. Louie and Kenny were disdainful of the UK press. They were the in-demand production duo / remixers who were overburdened in the studio, with fully booked touring and DJ schedules. As soon as we arrived at their office, they reduced the time previously agreed for the weekend session to a couple of hours total for the photographs and interviews. I'd flown four people all the way to New York for four days for an hour's work that could have been done on the phone. I had arrived unprepared for the weather and after taking the team for an evening with Roger Sanchez on the first night fell ill back at the Paramount Hotel. After a shopping trip to buy warmer clothing, I'd started coughing blood so called for a doctor who found that I was running a temperature just short of 40 degrees and I had contracted strep throat with bronchitis, both of which are highly contagious. I had no health insurance, a massive doctor's bill, was given antibiotics and quarantined for the weekend by the doctor. I was in hell, was panicking about being well enough to fly and I had no idea how best to resolve this.

Since the trip was now shorter than planned, one of the photographers asked to change their travel itinerary but this was declined by the press office back in London. My quarantine meant leaving the group to their own devices until the end of the trip, which also did not go down well. When we returned, I was chastised by the editor of *The Face* who reduced the feature length from four pages to half a column with a tiny press picture. I was hauled over the coals by the Head of Press for this expensive mistake and most of the expenses incurred remained unpaid on my credit card.

That same year, despite the unavailability of La India (the famous Puerto Rican salsa, house music and latin pop singer and the lead vocalist for Nuyorican Soul) and much random Miami Winter Music conference fall out, the team from *Dazed and Confused*[46] did a beautiful feature on her and the *Nuyorican Soul* album launch. In contrast, working with Terry Callier was like a soothing balm for the soul. Having been in the business since the seventies and understanding what was required, he was a dream to work with – and the only person who ever sent me a 'thank you' card.

As the Reprazent live tour sprang into action there were great reviews across the board. Their (and Kraftwerk's) first live festival gig at Tribal Gathering in the grounds of a country house in Luton Hoo on Saturday 24 May 1997 set the stage for an incredible summer. Things were looking good for the international leg. I took *Q Magazine* out to Japan to write an eight-page lead feature – we landed to find that Si John's double bass had broken in transit. At this point it didn't matter that they didn't have any TV or radio coverage because they were everywhere in the press. Their successful tour was well documented and the press campaign that I submitted to the Mercury Music Prize judging panel, which highlighted their evolution from the dance music weeklies to the national press, dailies and broadsheets, meant that they were shortlisted for the Mercury Music Prize.[47] In the run-up to the awards I sent regular press releases citing the betting odds. They started as 100–1 rank outsiders and closed at 16–1. Gilles Peterson, Paul Martin and I placed our bets at William Hill in Hammersmith and crossed our fingers.

When the win was announced[48] at the star-studded ceremony in The Grosvenor House Hotel, our senior managers took me to one side asking me to delay press comment so they could get their story straight. There was no stock in the distribution warehouses so no product available for the shops. They hadn't believed and were unprepared for the win.

My final year at Mercury was heavy going. Achievements were many but I had hit the glass ceiling. My press campaign was shortlisted for the Music Week Press Award but was beaten by Muff Fitzgerald's work for the Spice Girls, which naturally outshone all contenders. I thought it was a good time to pitch for promotion to a more senior role since I was already paid substantially above my pay scale, but I was talked out of it by the general manager and handed a meagre pay rise with no more responsibility. The glass ceiling was lead lined.

After the Mercury Music Prize, Reprazent were everybody's darlings. Daytime radio came on board, and they were on TV too. In addition to Roni Size and Reprazent's win, 4Hero were shortlisted for the Mercury Music Prize and gained a MOBO Award, while working with Terry Callier was an unforgettable, enriching life experience. My DJ'ing had a booster shot too as my 'Essential Mix' for Pete Tong's *Essential Selection* was broadcast on Radio 1. But in the office, my support network had fallen apart. Eddie

Gordon left, Gilles was under pressure, Paul Martin was on sick leave, the Black friends and colleagues I had, had all left and the atmosphere in the press department was toxic.

Kas Mercer's departure made for radical change in the press department. I was shocked when Angela (an over-eager, early applicant) called me for information about the vacancy for the Talkin' Loud Press Officer. It was clearly my job, but it had not yet been discussed with me. I addressed this and the situation in the press office with HR, requesting a transfer but there were no other posts available across the Polygram group. I interviewed with other record labels, securing firm offers from Virgin, ZTT and choosing the job with the most variety, scope and freedom, the joint role as Promotions and A&R Director with Azuli Records owned by David Piccioni and as the Press Officer for a start-up label called Defected Records, which was headed by Simon Dunmore, Janet Bell and Seamus Haji. On the day I left, I packed my three walls of framed magazine covers off to the respective bands as souvenirs. I was proud of my work and hoped they would be too. But my parting gift from the entire company was a petrol-station bought card, a £40 Harvey Nichols gift voucher and a bottle of Freixenet.

Working for Azuli and Defected presented me with a level of responsibility that was a welcome relief. Here I oversaw the promotion for two companies whose music was similar, the artists on the roster were mostly producers I knew, and I understood and was respected by the people and the culture implicitly. However, the companies were paced differently, the release schedules and work were time sensitive and confidential, and the businesses were situated across two different locations so I had to split myself mentally, physically and psychologically across the two offices. I pushed myself to the limit to do a week's work for each company in two and half days. At first it was thrilling. But after a year of revolving-door meetings[49] and scheduling madness, something had to give. I hadn't left Mercury to focus solely on organising publicity but Defected was quickly growing in stature and this was becoming likely. When Defected Records commissioned an independent PR company to take over the reins, the changeover was swift and I was free to focus on Azuli.

Created by (in his own words) 'a young skinny boy from Huddersfield', Azuli Records was a legendary independent record label with an iconic record shop beneath it,[50] both of which stand at the vanguard of house and electronic dance music history. In contrast to the luxury at Mercury Records, I had no company car but expenses were expected. It was not a modern office environment either but the community was family oriented. The townhouse rooms were cramped and open plan, the kitchen was tiny, while the ice-cold tap water and archaic phone system were not selling points. Upgrading it was part of mine and Jamila's[51] remit. Every day was like being let off a leash in a massive forest. I had a lot of territory to mark and a lot to learn. Being responsible for raising the profile and the bar for the label gave me the space to grow. David remarks:

> We were really not typical of the world out there. We played by a whole different set of rules and were not a good example for what was going on. While there was certainly a gender bias our community was multiracial. Outside it was a whole different era and not very pretty.
>
> We didn't strategise or think about it ... We just treated people right if they fitted or if they were right to work with us. We had a vast array of different kinds of characters. There weren't a lot of women around ... The breakthroughs in the DJ world like yourself, DJ Lottie and Sarah HB were unusual.

At my induction, David said that he would teach me everything about A&R. In interview I asked him what that 'everything' was and he replied:

> It's more what it wasn't [laughs]. There are so many records that I should have signed that I didn't because I listened to them in my office and not in a club ... Take Spiller from Rio – Spiller[52] bought the demo to me first but I played it in my office and played it in my car and felt that it was just another disco track. Then I DJ'ed with Spiller in a club in Italy. He played it and a thousand people went nuts. I tried to license it from him then, but he'd already signed it to someone else. You have to hear those tracks loud in a club ... and you have to be quick.

The biggest selling record on Azuli was Afro Medusa's 'Pasilda',[53] which I A&R'ed from a cassette tape played in the producer Mark Wilkinson's car while we took a break from the heat of the Lazy Dog[54] dancefloor one Sunday evening. As soon as I heard it, I knew it was a hit. I told Mark not to play it to anybody else and asked him to meet with me and David first thing on Monday morning. We had signed it by Monday afternoon. David comments:

> Afro Medusa was all down to you and full credit to you for bringing in Knee Deep[55] – something that you were totally responsible for. The proud moment for me – I was with my kids in the water park behind Space Ibiza and we'd just got to the top of the water slide when they played it and everyone started screaming at the breakdown.

My thoughts? Even though we had to license it on to the Ministry of Sound because it became too big for our label, I'm proud of putting the Afro Medusa package together. It's still being shown a lot of love twenty-two years later.

Through the noughties Azuli also found itself at the forefront of themed and branded compilation albums. We created the *Another Late Night* series, started the *Azuli Presents Choice* collections, and were the first dance music label to create branded destination compilations reflecting the releases associated with the Miami Winter Music Conference and Space Ibiza. I inspired, OK, pestered David to create the *Miami* series. We commissioned Lenny Fontana[56] to mix the first one and then I persuaded David to mix and produce the rest of the series himself. David says:

> You have to live the life when you're running a label. Things happen quickly. You have got to be really on it. With the albums as well as the singles, they just happened. They came from a place of really wanting to do it. Not for financial benefit, not because it was cool just because I really wanted to do it ... None of it was calculated.

And what else did I bring to the table? There was that time I tricked the management with my twin, Paula, in a Monday morning meeting (you should have seen their faces as the meeting ended when they saw the real me sitting at my desk in the office below). I wrote the *Azuli Presents Space* and *Miami* sleevenotes, and we had a glorious prime-time TV moment when *Miami Nice* aired on Channel 4.[57] I added retail radio to the promo remit organising guest mixes instore in HMV, Topshop and Selfridges for our roster of artists. I added student and foundling online radio stations and DJs to the mailing list and added new female DJs onto our database, one of whom was Nemone Metaxas.[58] I introduced marketing cards into all vinyl and CD releases so that we could build a long overdue consumer database. I commissioned the *Choice* sleevenotes from journalists with gravitas like Bill Brewster. I organised launch parties and Aids benefits on behalf of the label. It was a rapid-fire round and I left to conquer America in November 2001.

My introduction to the United States market came when I signed to Nervous Records for my *Must Be the Music* compilation mix album.[59] I was sofa surfing once again, this time in the downtown Chelsea apartment of Claudia Cuseta.[60] Once there, my A&R, Kevin Williams, introduced me to Michael Paoletta,[61] who booked me to speak on a panel at the Billboard Music Conference.⁶² On tour, I was delighted to head off through the opulence of Grand Central Station to visit the Yoshitoshi offices in Washington. It was exciting flying to San Francisco and walking down Sunset Boulevard in LA. Closing the tour at Centro Fly in New York was a dream. I DJ'ed for Nervous Records at their Armani Street parties and Denny's Breakfasts during the Miami Winter Music Conference, appearing alongside house-music royalty including Terry Hunter, Kenny 'Dope' Gonzalez, Dave Waxman and Tedd Patterson.

A few years later, David Perusse and Caroline Rousse – the creative directors and artist bookers for the magnificent Black & Blue Festival[63] in Montreal – had been invited to listen to DJ Colette at the Winter Music Conference but took a wrong turn, were intercepted by Kevin Williams and found themselves listening to me on stage at the Armani block party where we'd closed the street down. Of this, David Perusse says

> It was a definitive 'Click!' ... our relationship went pretty quick from there as we got you on board for 'Twist' (During Pride), which took place at the now defunct Club Med World venue during that same year. That was your first time spinning at one of our events ... while realising your set was way longer than anticipated[64] (on top of our very strong Montreal weed; HAHAHA!!!!). You managed it like butter and Montreal fell in love with you on the spot :) ... You then performed at the Main Event for the 2002 Black & Blue Festival which took place at the Olympic Stadium (Alongside Tom (Stephan), Mark (Anthony), Tracy (Young) and at the Main Event for the 2003 edition of Black & Blue with Tedd (Patterson).[65]

Touring the world was wild. Yet while dance music was exploding, the women were disappearing from the DJ charts. Even though Lottie was a firm fixture at Radio 1, when she won the Breakthrough DJ in *Muzik Magazine* and was

Welcome to the club

voted 50th in the *DJ Magazine* Top 100, she was only one of nine women to be included in the chart. While I was connected to some big brands and respectable agents there was a sea change coming. I joined David Dunne, Mark Ovenden, Gavin Kingsley, Robert Sharp and the team who created the Ministry of Sound online / DAB radio station in 2001 and was simultaneously contracted as a Ministry of Sound International Tours Resident. In the first year I played twenty-one dates around the world: my favourite territories were France, Spain, Ibiza, Switzerland, Russia, Prague, India and South America. I was tour managed by Gill Kingston for Asia and America, Caroline Stent for Europe, and Ian Mackley in Ibiza. We toured Asia and Las Vegas before they became the massive money pits they are now.

The Ministry of Sound tours[66] were selling well in Paris where I was requested for regular visits and radio show interviews, which I muddled through with my O Level French. I met Karim Ech-Choaby,[67] who invited me to shoot a feature for *Technikart*, a cool arts and culture magazine. I had already DJ'ed at a Paul and Joe[68] launch party in 1998 in Notting Hill and was invited to Paris to DJ for the opening of a new boutique in the Marais. Moving to Paris was becoming more attractive.

At his album launch for Defected Records, I sought advice from Martin Solveig – but he told me that moving to France wasn't a good idea. What did I do? I sold my London flat and moved to Paris in December 2004. I had no full-time job but my DJ diary was busy enough and having played with Didier Sinclair and Fafa Monteco I had discovered that they were both managed by a woman called Charlotte Lions at Enjoy Booking so I arranged a meeting.

*

It was January when we met at the Café Beaubourg across from the Pompidou Centre. I was dressed down in my customised army surplus jacket and trousers but like a true Parisienne Charlotte strode across the square, blonde hair shining in the sunlight, with a big fur coat that accentuated the space occupied, black cashmere jumper, black trousers and heels. She placed her Prada handbag in the middle of the table saying, 'I don't like women.' I was caught off-guard but the rest of the meeting went well, and I invited her to an intimate early evening party that I was throwing with my friend Fiona Coe at Andy Wahloo.[69] Charlotte arrived with Didier Sinclair who I found was the Head of Music at Radio FG and the top artist on her roster, and Ludovic Menard, who was then the creative director at Redlight.

I joined the Enjoy Booking roster and was booked by Charlotte for the duration of my time in France. With her I secured weekly residencies at Redlight, then Mix Club and in the final years held a bi-monthly residency at Queen Club. I toured largely alone, learning to speak French in the process and worked my way up to the highest level, sharing line-ups with the best that French house and electronic music had to offer. I was enough of a name to headline some of the biggest clubs and events on my own, winning 'Best DJ' awards in 2008 and 2010 voted by the public (with nominations in 2013 and 2014).

It's impossible to do my Parisian life justice in so few words. I clocked up at least 2,000 gigs, God knows how many air and TGV miles and 460 radio shows in that time. Beginning with Ministry of Sound international tours in 2004 and being given a police escort to the Solidays street parade playing to 30,000 people partying along the Seine in 2005 was like being shot out of a circus canon onto an unsuspecting public. Marche des Fiertés in the Place de la

Welcome to the club

Bastille was an annual highpoint, as was Technoparade and La Fête de la Musique, and I headlined them all regularly. I was so popular that people copied what I wore, how I looked. There was Paulettemania if they saw me shopping in Chatelet. Clubs placed metal barriers outside to restrain my fans from surging forwards as I entered. I released four compilation albums for Fashion TV and became one of their International Tour residents appearing in Bangkok, Egypt, Morocco, Kuala Lumpur, South Africa and playing dates all over France. I was employed as the Consultante Internationale at Radio FG head office, where I scouted my (English speaking) international DJ friends to record guest mixes and regular shows exclusively for the station. I curated and mixed a compilation for Mix Club, which was released on the underground electronic label Cyber[70] sold through FNAC (French equivalent to HMV), and the last compilation I curated for Radio FG and Toolroom Records. In 2010 it was one of Wagram's biggest selling CDs that year but it was only available in France. From 2008–10 I was responsible for filtering the promos in David Guetta's inbox (there are indeed witnesses to this). It was a full-time job done in only two days a week. From 2010 to 2013 I had a bi-monthly residency at Queen Club on the Champs Élysées where I could be seen smiling down onto the street like the Teletubbies sun every year on my birthday. When I left Paris for Ibiza, Cherie FM produced a short-form documentary on my leaving. This history is unknown outside France due to the language barrier, territory restrictions and media snobbery.[71]

Juice pre-series promo photo of Tara Newley, Johnny Dangerously and me, 1993

Me with my Dad standing outside the Free Trade Hall, Manchester on graduation day, 1994

Contact! Me with Edwin Starr and Roni Size representing at the Brit Awards, 1998

Me with Azuli Records crew at Hotel Es Vive in Ibiza, 2001. Back row (L to R): me, Zaki Dee, Nick Cran-Crombie. Front row: Dave 'Juggsy' Gardiner, Lewis Lenssen, David Piccioni

Me with Wendy Douglas and Anne Marie Bigby, London leaving party at The Friendship, Kensal Green, December 2004

So happy onstage at One Night with Paulette at Mix Club, Paris, 2007

A strong look

Channelling my inner Grace Jones

Up on the roof in La Défense with Vichy, a perfectly Parisian pooch. Dog and apartment courtesy of Sharmeen and Daniel Lalani-Fade

Who's going to know? Paula and me at St Kentigern's, aged eight

3
Bad behaviour: shit shags and crap hotels

Whenever anyone asks what I do for a living I proudly say, 'I'm a DJ.' I count to two, then it gets the raised eyebrow and 'that's so glamorous, I bet you live your life on Instagram / you've never done a day's hard work in your life / all you do is party all night and sleep all day'. I'd be lying if I said none of this has happened but accepting all of that would be downplaying the thousands of hours spent practising and honing my craft only to spend countless, mind-numbing hours in transit to get to that one gig. If you really want to know what DJs fees pay for, start here. Much of the time we're booked for is spent in preparation and in transit. It is a lonely pursuit and a pursuit for loners. From Monday to Sunday you prep – listening to hours of music, sending feedback forms, sorting the wheat from the chaff, digitising music, digging for music, making your own music. If you have a radio show this is the first stop for road-testing new music. From Friday to Monday, whether in first class or standard coach you wait, wasting valuable creative time by getting sucked into the travel vortex, buying stuff you don't need and bolting food you don't enjoy while working next to a power point that doesn't work or that you don't have the adapter for. You must love this job, as the law decrees that this is your daily lot. You pass on a delicious-looking portion of scampi and chips because you're on a healthy eating kick and will get a salad in the hotel. Then you are so delayed on the train that you will have to go straight to the club and all there is left in the basic café (when you risk leaving your seat) is yesterday's anaemic tuna and sweetcorn sandwich. The remaining hot option is a child-sized pizza, cut into quarters that's raw in the middle and has robbed you of £10.

Never doing a day's hard work would be discounting the times when we've lost the will to live, walking in an infinity loop around departure and executive lounges when 'delayed' escalates to 'cancelled' and you must find a way 'out of hours' to make the party happen. I have lost count of the times I've found myself poring over a departures board, in the middle of a grumpy, shouty crowd in packed French SNCF train stations mid-grève.[1] Living an Instagram life would forget the times bouncing over bumpy sand dunes in a 4x4 at speed, plastic bag in hand, travel sickness making a fool of me. It would make light of the packed or empty people carriers, the cars without snow tyres skidding on treacherous icy mountain roads, and the ferries when there's no other way to reach the stunning but remote and inaccessible venue.

'Never doing a day's hard work' would be erasing those times when I've sat on a plane, texting my agents and promoters to advise them that I've been blocked on a runway for three energy-draining, off-grid hours and I'm still there. Then there are the special occasions: birthdays, marriages, funerals, Christmas, New Year or Easter, when you leave your family behind to go to work surrounded by complete strangers or with FaceTime on hold in an empty room with Jools Holland's *Hootenanny* for company. It might not look

Welcome to the club

like work to the naked eye, but I guarantee you that the intensity and frequency of it is every bit as challenging.

Is this the glamorous life?

I pinch myself when I'm changing my clothes in a store cupboard that doubles up as the green room or when, for two hours, I am courteously shown to a waterlogged outdoor gazebo with three sidewalls flapping open and torrential rain lashing in. There's a full-length mirror without a stand, no solid furnishings to lean it on, no chair, no rider, no toilet nearby and no privacy. I laugh as I huddle in the corner to keep dry and warm until I'm called for my set. I hear you playing the smallest violin as I type, but I'm not being ungrateful. The truth is if you don't love this job, you won't last, as the glamour is fleeting, the graft is real, and the sacrifices are many.

While I love high-end service, I don't especially love hotels, as no matter how high the thread count, they are just rooms that other people have slept and behaved badly in. I love my own bed, and home is the sweetest place on earth. I find travel and experiencing different countries and cultures exhilarating but depending on the undisclosed (at time of booking) challenges of getting there and any unanticipated changes to the transfer schedule it can also make me wave my white flag. Most people only experience extreme travel situations when they take a holiday at peak season. Many people can work from home if there's a strike. These unhealthy peaks in cortisol levels happen every weekend and midweek for a busy DJ who might only work from home to record a live stream. While it's no excuse, it's no surprise that when the opportunity arises to release and let off steam, we will probably get leathered. Wouldn't you?

As a follow on from Flesh, Paul Cons and Lucy Scher launched a mixed gay / straight night at Tom Bloxham's new nightclub called HOME[2] in Manchester. I'd DJ'ed at the launch party and had been chosen to host the second room for their party called 'The World'. As I'd taken two months off from DJ'ing to sit my finals and concentrate on presenting the TV programme *Juice*, my first night out after graduation and the series wrap was bookmarked for THE liberation celebration.

We'd bought everything we needed in advance and stocked the fridge with goodies. There were jellies made with overproof Vodka that took ages to set; Gary had brought enough weed to start an Amsterdam Koffee Shop, and B had a Skittles-looking assortment of pills in his pockets. There was so much stuff to get through that we started after dinner. B and J tricked one of my friends into taking her ecstasy pill before anyone else. The pill kicked in quickly. The party at HOME didn't start until 10 p.m. so obviously no one wanted to leave the house before 8 p.m. The Kingsway didn't play house music and we had no reason to go to Dry Bar 201. My friend was itching to dance while the rest of us (who hadn't taken any ecstasy yet) were cosily getting stoned, talking and listening to music. Now we were riding the rave Push Me-Pull You. After stalling for an hour my friend impatiently said she would go into town on her own. 'OK let's go,' I said. 'Now who's driving?' After some debate and a group sober test we arrived at the club at 9.20 p.m. then spent forty minutes in the empty car park dancing to tunes on the car radio until the manager arrived to open and let us in.

By 11 p.m., my room was packed, I was focused on my set, and everyone was having a great time. Then B handed me a pill. I had no pockets, and since the security were standing to the side of the DJ booth, I took the whole pill rather than leave it in view on the mixer. Taking a whole ecstasy

Welcome to the club

tablet was a bold move for me since I am incapacitated after 'having a nibble' or sharing one between four. Just as I swallowed it, I caught sight of my friends who were all slowly melting into the pillars that were supporting them. 'Shit, shit, shit,' I whispered.

Soon after, every record and sleeve turned black with no discernible print or title to differentiate one from another. Since I organise my record box alphabetically, I guessed where records were, previewing the tracks in my headphones. This worked well until my hearing started cutting out just as I was bringing the mix across. A volcanic pressure had started to build in my body which I tried hard to control. 'Are you ok?' chuckled J. I smiled weakly, knowing full well that I wasn't. My twin, Paula, was dancing and blowing her whistle as loudly as she could, oblivious to my distress. There was such a great atmosphere in the room that nobody noticed me struggling, huffing or puffing, and sitting down on my record box with my head in my hands after each successful selection. At midnight I played Donna Giles, 'And I'm Telling You I'm Not Going', and I went to join my friends in the dance. I was ecstatic, lifted and soaring on thermals like a bird to the music. I wanted to dance more but where was the DJ? I forced myself back behind the decks but playing records had now become an effort with a capital E'd up. Then came the inconvenient part. I needed to get small in a large room that was packed with dancing, sweating people.

Oh dear.

Since I could no longer fight the fog, I asked Paula (my wildcard) and J (completely mangled but with some knowledge of how to work the DJ setup) to cover for me while I got my head together in private. It was genius. It made perfect sense to dupe a dark room full of serious ravers with my identical twin. Who's going to know?

Bad behaviour

Paula had never DJ'ed before and dropping her in at the deep end means that she probably never will again. While she loves and understands music and can make mixtapes with her eyes closed, she says that she had zero aptitude and no desire to do what I do in a nightclub. Unfortunately for me, J and Paula were the only choice since my remaining friends (who were living their best lives) looked as if they were sharing one brain cell between them.

Safe in a cubicle, the metal toilet-roll dispenser became my pillow. The strains of Dawn Penn's 'No, No, No' drifted into the toilet with each opening of the door. The first time they played it, it received a rapturous cheer. The second time there was no cheer and by the third, the hum of the buzzing room had significantly died down. What could I do? I was sledged[3] and rocking in my 'club for one' where the buzz of the bass was vibrating onto my forehead.

Paula knocked on the toilet door: 'Are you alright? when are you coming back?' I felt like my head was screwed on back-to-front. 'In a minute,' I said, grinding my teeth. She replied, 'Well, if you're alright can I go back? J's playing Judy Cheeks and it's my turn to play it next.' It took three more partial plays of Judy Cheeks's single 'Reach' before I stumbled out of the toilets, to find my friend Lucy blocking people from leaving the room promising, 'Don't go, they'll get good in a bit'. They never did.

Back in the DJ booth my legs betrayed me. B caught me, then carried me with as little fuss as possible out of the room through the bar area and up the stairs delivering me into a taxi outside. I made a mumbled apology on my way out to Paul Cons, promising that I would be back and better next week. He was thankfully understanding. At the door, our guestlist person, Jasen Grindrod, was less so, hooting hysterically after me, 'Ooooo gave 'errrr a pill.'

Welcome to the club

As soon as I lay down at home, I was ok. Assured that I felt fine, B tucked me in and went back to the club, and I spent the early hours of the morning climbing a tree, shaking the branches to get the fruit, and talking to the leprechauns that had gathered below. I was happily hallucinating when everyone got back from the club, so we partied a bit more then I passed out, boots on, fully clothed and rigid as a rake after taking a yellow Temazepam that I had been told was only mild. I learned that day that I have a low tolerance for drugs: prescription and illegal. But that didn't stop me trying them again.

Twice a year, from the late 1980s through to the mid-2010s, the Southport Weekender was THE annual event, descended on by all the key music-industry pluggers, A&Rs, radio and TV presenters and DJs where the producers and record labels showcased their upcoming productions and releases. This Ainsdale Butlins camp takeover was an important networking opportunity and the place where many deals were struck. Me, B, J and some other friends had booked in for the weekend, staying in a hotel close by, but many of our friends had chalets on site. The Friday night was mellow, spent acclimatising, exploring the rooms, finding out who was there and getting briefly up to no good in a chalet with a humming cooker switch, which ended the party early.

Saturday night was a different beast. The Powerhouse backstage area was heaving with talent. Roger Sanchez and Todd Terry were playing material that we were all trying to take note of. There was no Shazam, we had no recording devices, mobiles or PDAs and the noise of chatter and everyone comparing notes was deafening. There was one toilet in this crowded room, and it was always occupied. Someone offered me a bump that I assumed was cocaine.

Bad behaviour

It was not cocaine. Whatever-it-was-that-was-not-cocaine kicked my ass just as I and my friend Leo were dancing, hidden from view. I tripped over a random ladder, falling through the curtains as Todd Terry played onstage in the Powerhouse. We landed laughing in a heap behind him and were quickly banished from the area.

We annoyed people like that until six in the morning. How we got back to the hotel is anybody's guess since we were flying. Back in the room, it was a drain-the-minibar, curtains-closed, no-sleep lock-in that went on longer than it should have. Just as we decided to call it a day and grab some sleep, a noise punctured the fragile calm. The sound was so invasive that I hid in the bath with the towels over my head, while B tried to cover the smoke detector with a towel. The pitch intensified. It was so unbearable that we searched under every piece of furniture for an abandoned alarm clock. It wasn't that. It was only when I opened the curtains and saw the entire clientele of the hotel gathering in the car park below when I realised that a real fire drill was in motion.

Choices. Straighten up and fly right or burn to death sniffing the cocaine you have spilled on the carpet while ignoring the fire alarm? Choose wisely. It might save your life.

We packed, checked out of the hotel feeling frazzled and bedraggled then made our way to the Pizza Hut where I sent everything I ordered back twice before realising that it was my tastebuds that were at fault. Contrite and sleep deprived, the rest of Sunday was spent chilling then watching The Sounds of Blackness in The Powerhouse. We sang along to Optimistic and The Pressure and cried tears of joy because (as we said sobbing) music can do that to you whether you're on drugs or not.

Paul and Lucy ran a smaller Saturday party called The Glory Hole. Based at Bar Kay[4] it was a hype gay spot where me, Matt Ryan and Kath McDermott played house and disco to a lively crowd. I give the Glory Hole this special mention because my mum Blanche was my costume collaborator, roadie and record box carrier, and she became the Queen of the dancefloor. Whenever she danced, she was flanked by gorgeous, tops-off men. She was curious why people put a brown bottle to their noses to smell a weird perfume that she thought smelled like sweaty socks. 'That's poppers ... amyl nitrite,' I said as if it was a perfectly normal thing to tell your mum. 'But why sniff it when it smells so bad. It stinks?' she said. 'It's a relaxant that makes their E work quicker,' I replied a little too knowledgeably. My mum graduated from Oxford in 1972 but I guess we can all learn something from each other.

Every week we had a lock-in after closing, where we set up the decks and monitors in the courtyard behind the DJ booth and a select group of people who'd stayed behind danced to my music on the fire escapes of the surrounding buildings into the early hours. It was surreal and beautiful. This took us nicely to Oscars where, with mum still in tow, we could get afterhours alcohol and some of us managed a breakfast. My mum loved Oscars because the proprietor, Bubbles, always made a fuss of her. If we didn't go to Oscars, there was always an after party to be found in India House.[5] My mum sometimes came along to the parties there, but she could never understand why people politely refused the sandwiches she made. I have a cool – and sometimes beautifully naive mum.

I have been on more road trips with Gary than any other friend. This is what happened on our first, a Manchester to Brighton run. My club residency began in June 1994 and by July – after commuting from Manchester every weekend[6] – I decided it would make life much easier if I moved to

Bad behaviour

London. It took me just over a month to find a basement flat across from Hyde Park and the Lancaster Hotel in Bayswater and my moving-in weekend was 6 August. Since it coincided with my Zap residency, Gary's plan was to pack my stuff in the car, drive to Brighton, I DJ – he enjoys the night – then we'd drive to London on Sunday and offload my gear, thus saving me the van hire. I had a twin room every Saturday at The Sheridan Hotel so it was easy to break the journey.

On moving day we filled his estate car with my Technics Turntables, TEAC amps, Celestion Speakers, KAM Made 2 Fade GMT03X, speaker stands, two beds, a TV, assorted tables, books, binbags full of clothes and shoes, videos, a VHS player, an Atari computer, some kitchenware and lots of vinyl. I didn't think I had that much stuff, so how we fitted in once the car was loaded was anybody's guess.

The drive passed smoothly but as we reached the seafront, we were confronted with a mass of white vans and a police control. The roundabout wasn't cordoned off and the road had not been diverted. As we waited in the traffic queue, we heard rumblings about a bomb scare. Impatient with the tailback, Gary drove round the roundabout near the fun fair, along Kings Road pursued by the police, then parked up outside The Sheridan Hotel to drop me off. He reasoned with the policeman that he had the right to do so because I was an important DJ who had a gig at the Zap under the arches directly across from the hotel. He said that I was moving to London and he had a car full of my stuff that needed storing safely out of the way. Whatever situation it was must have been cleared because the policeman waved Gary on without a caution or a fine. Later that night we were told that there had been a serious bomb scare three days before[7] but thankfully this secondary situation was a false alarm and the Zap raved on.

Welcome to the club

Through the nineties and noughties the dance music magazines turned the tabloid Leah Betts / Summer of Love bad press on its head to create caner culture.[8] Drug taking was cool again, immortalised on Hysteric Glamour T-shirts while *Mixmag* published separate issues with Speed, Ecstasy and Trips on the cover. *Muzik* magazine included a 'Caner of The Year' Award in its annual 'End of the Year' gong show. The *Face* editorial and 'ladmags' like *Loaded*, *FHM*, *Maxim*, *Nuts* and *Zoo* used the criteria of how delicately or indelicately wasted celebrities got to rank the most beautiful women and the coolest men. Everywhere you looked, the media was encouraging bad behaviour that, as impressive as it was to read, would soon be to the detriment of the health of the people it celebrated. Norman Cook, Derek Dahlarge, Brandon Block, Nicky Holloway and Dave Beer all benefited from the regular column inches, continuing to work successfully through their blunder years. But during the 1998 Radio 1 Weekend in Ibiza, Zoe Ball narrowly missed a serious reprimand after pulling an all-nighter before getting to the studio on time for her show (but being sick in a dustbin two minutes before going on air). Not everyone avoids disgrace. The same weekend Andy Parfitt[9] fired Lisa I'Anson for missing her show, going AWOL in Manumission and being incomprehensible when located. Daniella Westbrook's coke-burnt septum was front-page tabloid news, yet men's bad behaviour was rarely commented on unless somebody was found handcuffed to a bed or if they ran their car into a Snappy Snaps window. We're expected to have it large but when the dust gathers we can never be the heroes that men are. There is a definite gender bias in how this behaviour is accepted and reported.

I had no fear of ending up in the tabloids with my track record. Still, I made multiple trips to Ibiza with the Manifesto records team under the auspices of showing journalists how important our music was out there. The senior management did not agree with or understand Eddie Gordon's logic in promoting music like this so refused to fully finance our trips but that did not deter us. Each prospective department covered the flights, then we all ordered 'giveaways' that we took with us – and sold on a makeshift stall at the entrance to Amnesia[10] to fund the villa, food and everything else we required for the week. In the same year that we launched our African artist Indo's album at Café Del Mar we threw a huge party at Cream in Amnesia.

In the excitement of arriving in Ibiza airport and the confusion of getting luggage and renting hire cars, nobody realised that we'd left Anne Marie Bigby[11] at the airport until the 'Where's Kevin'[12] penny dropped and one of the team drove back to the airport to collect her. The roads then were narrow dirt tracks with no safety barriers. Unused to driving in Europe we occasionally drove cars the wrong way or at night-time veered off the unlit roads into the rocky ditches below. At Cream in Amnesia I had the honour of DJ'ing with Norman Jay and Andy Carroll on the terrace while the Manifesto A&R department – Luke Neville and Judge Jules – played the main-room sets. Come to think of it, I didn't receive a single peseta for that gig either. It was at Café Del Mar that I first got wasted on *hierbas*[13] and *lumumba*.[14] And it was in Amnesia where I took my first dab of brown MDMA[15] from a vintage powder compact.

Drink and drugs and the misuse thereof have long been the bedfellows of artists in the music industry. From Billie Holiday to Dinah Washington, from Miles Davis to John Coltrane, from Jimi Hendrix to Joe Cocker, from Lou Reed to David Bowie, from Amy Winehouse to Avicii, from Prince to Michael Jackson and Mac Miller – alcohol, opiates,

Welcome to the club

barbiturates, opioids and prescription drugs have accompanied the spectacular highs and been the basis for the tragic addictions and incredible lows of our finest artists. Over the years, documentaries like Channel 4's *Miami Nice*, *This Is Ibiza*, *Ibiza Drugland* and *White Island* have investigated and addressed it; they also backhandedly glamourised it.

Is this the glamorous life?

It's reported that Annie Nightingale treasures the gong that the dance magazine *Muzik* awarded to her for 'Caner of the Year' in 2001. When she asked what she had done to deserve it she was told: 'Everywhere we've been partying, you've been there. Miami, Ibiza – for dedication to the cause.' Then 61, she had chalked up more than thirty years at BBC Radio 1, but the caner award was special to her because it acknowledged her standing in dance music – the genre to which she has dedicated herself since the late eighties and saw her gaining the respect of a new generation of fans. 'That one [is my favourite honour],' she said. 'Wouldn't it be yours?'[16]

Around this time[17] I'd organised a Joey Negro[18] album launch / listening party for the Azuli released album *Can't Get High Without You* at Caroline Prothero and DJ Lottie's mythic (Thursday is the new Saturday) 'Missdemeanours' party at AKA.[19] As always, 'Missdemeanours' was a fabulously excessive session that culminated in only a few hours' sleep before work the next morning. I was so hungover that I couldn't focus on my computer. Everyone else in the office had left early so felt fine, but I had DJ'ed after Dave Lee and stayed till the bitter end. I put all calls on hold to hide underneath my desk, summoning death but death would not come. My masterstroke was remembering that I had booked an Azuli A&R management meeting at Busaba on Wardour Street for Friday afternoon at one o'clock. The vibrant buzz, warm wooden tones and viscous, spicy aromas worked their magic on my stubbornness to let everything go. After picking at my favourite calamari and green peppercorns starter, I absented myself from the meeting, reaching the bathroom just in time to say hello to everything I'd taken and drunk the night before. I met my edge and investigated the abyss there.

Apart from Annie Nightingale in 2001, female caners are not habitually respected or fêted. It's not a good look for a woman to be seen to have lost control or be photographed looking twisted behind the decks. I am normally a control freak about my behaviour in public but there have been occasions ...

Presenting at a major TV channel interview with a well-known electronic duo's last gig at Alexandra Palace is the least favourite leg of my drugs journey. A people carrier transported me and my guests from my apartment to the event, but when we arrived at Alexandra Palace our reception was not as expected. I, and my guests, were shown to a small, bare dressing room with no windows and no hospitality or entertainment (other than the cocaine and banter that my friends had brought with them) for three hours. We were not allowed to join the crowd or stand backstage and enjoy the set of the pre-concert DJ as it was a live broadcast.

The devil makes work for idle hands. Without realising, we took everything we had. When I was eventually called to take my place on the spot from which I would enter the stage on the AP's cue I was coked and stoked but ready. As I waited in the dark, the AP missed the cue to send me onstage to announce the band. I signalled to check, just as he was talking into his walkie-talkie. The band rushed past me to take to the stage and the DJ (who was then leaving the stage) grabbed the mic from the AP and announced the band instead of me then rushed offstage. The AP had no explanation or apology. It was like a bullet had ripped through my brain.

The job I'd waited three hours to do had been botched. Any other day, I'd have been reasonable – you have to be on live TV. Live programmes have to appear seamless so when mistakes are made you move on so that nobody can see the tear. But I had cocaine running around my brain. Like David Banner[20] I threw a spectacular out-of-body tantrum: swearing, effing, jeffing, shouting, kicking and slamming everything. I nearly broke my foot kicking the reinforced dressing room door. It was me, but it wasn't me. It took a long time to calm me down then we had to wait until the end of the gig to go home. Despite my efforts to apologise, I never worked for that TV station again and I'm not proud of that.

Fortunately, my DJ schedule was hectic and I'd started to work in the USA. Across the Atlantic, Montreal events provided many off-the-wall and unorthodox moments that make me laugh even today.

Occasionally, when the spirit takes me, I leave the DJ booth to dance or vibe with the crowd at the front of the stage. It became a repeat occurrence when every year when I appeared at the Black & Blue Festival 'Main Event' I was ejected by security who somehow weren't aware that I – the DJ and the person on the stage – were the same person. This happened three years running, twice in the Stade Olympique before 28,000 people and once at the Palais De Congres in front of 14,000 people. I don't think there are many headliners who get bum-rushed off their own stage at the peak of the party.

I'd wanted to play at Stereo[21] for years, it being one of the 'bucket list' clubs for any ambitious house music DJ. One year, when I was booked to play at the Leather Ball (again for the Black & Blue Festival) my flight from London was severely delayed. I arrived in Montreal at 8.30 p.m. instead of 2.30 p.m., which left me with no time to rest. My set that evening was to start at 9.30 p.m. and I was to DJ until 4 a.m. or 6 a.m. depending on the crowd. Stereo does not serve alcohol, but I was so badly jetlagged that the organisers brought me some vodka in Dasani water bottles and a joint. I got so stoned and drunk that I barely remember what I played but the dancefloor was solid all night and I took a great picture of the sound system. Drinking what I thought was water from the Dasani bottle on my bedside table was not the wake up I'd intended. Stereo was memorable but not for the reasons I'd hoped. Then there was the funny gig at Sona when David Perusse and I were a little bit 'dazed', sitting on the floor in the production office laughing our heads off while trying to count my fee which had been paid in an incredible amount of $1 bills. How many recounts?

My inability to take or supply enough drugs and party hard enough meant that I couldn't keep up with the people who could. I was never a confident or comfortable guest at afterparties. I knew that drugs made me unpredictable plus the comedowns made me bad tempered and disorganised. I kept trying to fit in but with less and less success. So it was a relief when I moved to France and found that it was not the same hardcore 'any day that ends in a Y, all week, every weekend' drug culture as it was in London. The people I was around had small apéros, big dinner parties, drank wine and champagne, smoked weed (if they did drugs at all) or only took class A drugs on special occasions. The apparent scarcity of drugs and dealers here meant that this was THE place to get shitfaced on wine, champagne and numerous other overproof digestifs instead.

I've played, eaten and drunk my way around the main French departments at least five times (probably more).

Welcome to the club

I've learned how to take caramel vodka shots in Strasbourg- (standing with my hands behind my back, bend like an emu, pick the glass up with my mouth, swallow shot in one, slam glass down on the bar). I've OD'd on Poire Williams digestif in Dijon, passing out in the hotel after dinner after having already been sick, only to wake up with a pre-gig hangover ten minutes before the pick-up arrived for the party. I DJ'ed with a bucket under the console just in case. I grew to love L'Hortus Pic St Loup in Montpellier and drank copious 'piscines'[22] in Cannes, Nice and Monaco. Come to think of it, I was perma-pissed for nearly ten years, to the point of having a weekly order of red, white and champagne and a much-used loyalty card for the wine retailer, Nicolas.

The annual Foire Aux Vins in Colmar is a mecca for wine aficionados. It closes with a huge party, 'La Nuit Blanche', where in 2009 I supported David Guetta at the 10,000-capacity sold-out event. Nobody told me it was a White party and I'd worn the most colourful dress I could find. David Guetta arrived wearing head to toe black, so I didn't feel so bad. I was briefed what I could play before and after his set – then I topped and tailed his performance. The party was a great success and everybody was happy. Of course, I mixed my drinks and got hideously drunk because that's what the 'Foire Aux Vins' is also all about.

Next morning, I found myself fending off the advances of an overzealous 'coup d'un soir'[23] before the train departed. Just as I thought I'd escaped, he jumped the train without paying and sat next to me in a closed carriage. Hungover and easily persuaded, I went against my better judgement and found myself negotiating his rampant hormones in a moving TGV toilet. The constant flushing of the metal tank with its industrial strength Bloo was not aphrodisiac to me so the frantic knocking of the train controller was a welcome intervention. I opened the door and mumbled, 'J'ai très mal au ventre',[24] then faux-retched, to explain why there was a man in the toilet with me. The controller left us alone – I guessed correctly that he wouldn't watch me vomit. Mr CDS was ejected in Strasbourg as he didn't have a ticket to ride. Not with me and not with SNCF. Take my advice: loneliness, a hangover, beer glasses, bad decisions and an early train or plane are never a good combination.

Other things to avoid are the hotels that give that sinking check-in feeling: you know, the sense of melancholy you get when your room smells of stale cigarettes, wet dogs, old wee and serial killings. The rooms that have no mini-bar and a trouser press or a travel iron with half the carpet melted onto it are a luxury. I've stayed in miniscule rooms in Dijon and Montpellier, in Reims, Rennes, Grenoble and Aix En Provence with heavy seventies wooden furniture, six clashing textile patterns, pathetic two-cup kettles and mini plastic cups in plastic wrap, which make you feel like you tore the space–time continuum when you opened the door. I'm tired of whizzing off toilets with thin, wobbly seats that were only secured in place by the plastic 'sanitised today' strip. I say 'no' to bath towels that barely preserve your dignity and shower curtains that rarely cover the bath and as for the tsunami that seeps into the bedroom carpet from shower heads that have zero water pressure control – how does this even happen? I've checked straight out of supposed 4-star hotels with a double bed the size of a toothpick. The disappointment there came for free along with the low-grade Lipton tea bags, cubed sugar, one individually packed Biscoff and milk in thimble-sized pots.

It was nearly six hours from Paris to Gruissan by TGV and it took another forty minutes to drive to the hotel. Shattered from the journey, the scenic beauty of the *Betty*

Welcome to the club

Blue fishing village was marred by the dodgy lodgings. The hotel room was barely a double with its bed like a box of matches, faded lilac polycotton sheets and a Twiglet for a pillow. The shower scalding hot, induced an immediate blister on my hand. I'd forgotten the lock code to my new iPhone, the hotel had a landline but no service to call / email Orange to unblock it. There was no First Aid kit, no TV, no kettle or free biscuit, no dining room and no room service. There was nowhere close by to get a snack after 6 p.m. and no one on reception after 7 p.m. Dinner had been booked for 11 p.m. I know exactly why *Betty Blue* lost the plot. The depression soaked into my bones like ink through litmus.

Although hotel misrepresentation can cause pain, nothing triggers me more than technical breakdowns: they are my ultimate Achilles heel. We travel now to Paris in 2011 for an unforgettable snafu that has scarred me deeply.

Along with Marche des Fiertés, La Fête de la Musique and Technoparade, Radio FG's annual party in the Virgin Megastore on the Champs Élysées[25] was a highlight in the Parisian electronic music calendar. For this event, Bob Sinclar was headlining, and I was closing, while French stars Hakimakli, Norman Doray and Tristan Garner were slated to appear before me. I'd played in this splendid location with its opulent marble sweeping staircase every year since 2008; I knew it instinctively, but tonight there was feedback, the mics kept cutting out and there were random volume surges. While this worried me, it was washing over the technical team like water.

As I approached the DJ booth, Tristan Garner whispered that only two CDJs were working. This was still doable I thought, three is better but you can still play with two. Then as we handed over, Tristan whispered, 'That was a nightmare, now only one CDJ is working.' I cued my first CD – it started OK. The cheers erupted. Then the music ground to a halt. I pressed play. Nothing. I pressed play on the second deck. Nothing. I cleaned the CD and tried to fire it again. Nothing. I tried a CD in Deck 3. Nothing. Now I was starting to panic. A continuous DJ mix requires two turntables or one CDJ and one vinyl in operation to work. One-deck play is reserved for home listening, album playbacks or intimate bar sessions. I could have got round it if I'd had one working CDJ and a pre-prepared mix handy, but since no machine was operational even that wouldn't have saved me or this event.

The crowd, impatient to continue the party, was starting a slow handclap. The head of the radio station now aware of the lack of music, came into the booth to ask why the music had stopped. I explained that none of the equipment was working and asked if there were replacement CDJs on site or if there was a sound engineer available. He laughed. The engineer had left when Bob Sinclar's set had finished. Now people were starting to boo. I asked the event manager if he could make an announcement as my French wasn't fluent enough to placate an angry crowd. He joked, 'Why don't you sing instead?'

This was a Parisian midweek session. I wasn't drunk, I wasn't high, and his suggestion did not land well. I told him to 'take the mic and sing yourself', then grabbed my headphones and stepped down off the stage. He made the announcement, and the party was over. But in the fallout, I was deemed to be an 'être de mauvaise foi'.[26] That curse of Black women for speaking out of turn and seen to be behaving badly.

Mentioning the word 'Ibiza' elicits a Pavlovian response from all: it's 'that non-stop party island where they do a lot of drugs' and I have to agree. It was here where I left Pacha in such a state that I fell asleep on the floor outside the apartment one storey beneath where I was staying because my key (obviously) didn't work. I've played extended sets on the old Space Terrace because the DJ following me was too spannered to see and couldn't play. I've seen the dirty Panda Woman of Old Ibiza town join the dancers on the podium, lip syncing to The Supermen Lovers, 'Starlight' on Space Terrace. It was such a kooky happening that I wrote it into the sleeve notes of the Azuli Ibiza 2001 compilation.

The bad behaviour wasn't always mine though. It was Ibiza where the aperitif shots at a staff party were heavily spiked and not everyone was in on the joke. It's here where I was held up by the throat in a VIP area by a notoriously psychotic promoter who took his rage out on me because the creative team at the Parisian club I was resident at had not booked his brand for a party five years prior. I've giggled with young French men in leopard print posing pouches and I've played Agony Aunt to bed buddies who have never slept with a Black woman before. I've fought off predatorial Germans-on-Viagra at villa parties. I've run from sad little Napoleons who celebrated their conquest by wearing their Superman nightgown to dinner (I didn't stay for dessert). I've listened to sex addicts and married men whimpering tedious monologues of loyalty, secrecy, apology and regret while racking out lines in their cars. One creep had the cheek to verify my age (it was forty-seven) against my passport. I left immediately after. In the search for that elusive stability I've kissed more frogs and dogs than is good for me. I put those experiences in the bin where they belong.

There will always be a crutch you can lean on to get you through. If we are smart, we opt for the positive ones like yoga, meditation, mindfulness, swimming, running, walking, sport or therapy. Unfortunately, gaming, gambling, food, alcohol, drugs and sex are the quicker fix when you're playing away. You can get anything online. Most good hotels or artist liaisons have access to them or have numbers. Choices, choices, choices.

Where sex, drugs and rock and roll intersect, becoming central to most DJs resumés, I'm the odd one out. I've lain on pebbles as the tide has come in, convinced I'm luxuriating on an Axminster carpet. I've taken lines of cocaine off the highly mirrored wedged heel of a now collectable Prada shoe that was passed under a toilet door. I'm glad that I managed to rein it in before it became too damaging though. I have my own teeth, a clean bill of physical and sexual health, a divorce but no kids and apart from a few misguided cocaine-fuelled meltdowns, have a clear conscience. Making my peace with the solitary nature of this DJ life, finding myself by stopping trying to fit in with people or in places where I no longer fit, accepting my limitations with drugs, and finding sobriety has been a slow process that continues but is absolutely worth the effort.

4

FAQs (female asked questions)

> And the risk to remain tight in a bud was more painful than the risk it took to blossom.
>
> – Anaïs Nin

Nothing says winter or Christmas at your mum's quite like a comforting bed with a crisp white bedspread and a king-sized double duvet all tucked in, a dresser with its porcelain saucer filled with multicoloured potpourri and a bottle of iced water beading around it. It's all there to greet me when I arrive back in Manchester, and as a bonus my mum has proudly made my Year 2 primary-school 'How We Used to Live' project the centrepiece. Through its yellowing pages I could still make out where my teacher had triumphantly marked A+ in red biro. She had marked it on the page which was headed '1918 – The Suffragettes – Votes for Women'.

I've always been fascinated, surrounded and inspired by strong, vocal women. My mother, Blanche (who deserves an award) was a working wife and, for the most part, single mother who balanced her full-time job as Equal Opportunities Officer at Manchester City Council with university studies, a part-time job as Northern Branch Secretary for Equity and a night-time job either running her co-owned nightclub or singing jazz and cabaret as 'Blanche

FAQs (female asked questions)

Finlay' with her band The Prophets in clubs, pubs and festivals around the country. She set a high standard, while keeping us sheltered, clothed and fed. I, my twin, my five older sisters and brother – Paula, Elizabeth, Audrey, Elicia, Jennifer, Rhonda and Robert – progressed through the education system as far as we could, then found full-time jobs, often holding down more than one. In our house, Black women's / people's rights were an everyday concern: my mum was always having militant letters published in *The Times* or reading our head teachers the Riot Act.

I was prepared for the world, mentored by right-on feminists. Through them I learned that independent, multi-skilled and mature people are Swiss Army-knife useful and a valued member of any team. They enable every community to be well rounded, capable of completing any task and building entire villages and cities without having to outsource jobs. For us, being a 'Jack of all trades' was a reality not a judgement.

I have long been aware that there is a marked difference in the way that Black women are allowed to occupy space in the workplace, and how white women with less experience can earn more and scale the ladder more quickly, and the overarching privilege that most white men have, at every level, of comfortably being there and getting everywhere with the least amount of effort, encouraged, allowed and expected to achieve, and promoted easily when they do.

The stigma of difference and the assumption that the simplest of tasks – and life – is harder for a woman, perfumes everything we do. To be equal we must do more. No matter what nationality we are or which country we reside in – no matter how young, how old, or how different we are as people or how varied we are musically, as DJs we face the same, tired questions concerning the gendered challenge of being capable of doing anything at all. Intrigued by the idiocy of this, I gathered some friends together to dissect and examine the issues, stereotypical attitudes, and the standard female DJ interview questions.

The most asked (and most detested) question is 'is it hard being a female DJ'. This is like a red rag to a bull. In the beginning, 'DJ' wasn't a career ambition or goal for anyone (men included) so we women never saw our gender, race or sexuality as compromising it any further. It is a job that we all naturally fell into through our passion for music, the love of people and clubbing and the obsession (perhaps nerdiness!) of record collecting. We honed our craft as everyone else did, learning on the job, practising at home, buying our own equipment and improving over time. We didn't do it to be famous or to get more followers and likes. We did it for love. We did it for the party. Marcia Carr remembers her start:

> I'd be the one farsing with the radiogram – the one who they would call on for family functions. I was at college, 16/17 years old, and I always got called on to play the music. One day I thought, 'I can do what those guys are doing.' I'd been DJ'ing at college, then I found myself playing at Busby's.

A violinist is a violinist, a pianist is a pianist, a guitarist is a guitarist, a musician is a musician. When people ask me what I do for a living, I say, 'I am a DJ.' I don't feel I need to make any other distinction. Gender makes no difference to the way we do or should classify this job. Technically DJ'ing doesn't require any skills that are specific to either sex when they perform. We do the same job and use the same equipment and materials. There is no heavy lifting or brute force required (apart from lugging boxes of vinyl around) yet it is segregated, and remunerated, as if there is. The job has been gendered in speech, flyers, interviews and pay, and this perpetuates the 'novelty' aspect which over time has become entrenched.

No matter what gender we are or choose to be, we inherit twenty-three chromosomes from each parent, so by rights we should all be equal. Wrong. It was 2019 when Anz[1] enlisted me for a chat with Tash LC on Red Bull's 'Normal Not Novelty'[2] workshop for women and non-binary artists in Leeds. The prefix DJ'ette / DJane / SheJ / Female DJ as a marketing category accentuates our otherness and makes the profession harder to equalise, while scarcity and low visibility puts men higher in the booking and line-up order. This summer I was approached by a woman whose boyfriend (the 'promoter') had booked me for their party in Manchester. She was shocked and intrigued to hear me play because in the years of their running that party they had never booked a female DJ. The education and ministry continue.

We are the pioneers, the foot soldiers who struck out alone into uncharted territory, keeping a few steps ahead of the rest, striding over rough terrain, inadvertently or intentionally clearing the path for others to follow. We founded a new culture, and a new way of life, then shared our love, vision, desire and the obsession that drives us generously with the world. With no one like us who we could model ourselves on, we became the influencers and influences of the future. But pioneers rarely get the recognition they deserve.

Marcia Carr reflects: 'For us [Black women] coming through and having zero influences – it was hard to become something that you can't see.' Among my interviewees, the lack of female role models (specifically for DJs but also in management and booking) is almost unanimously voiced but Kath McDermott cites Manchester in the nineties as an exception. Here, her experience of living in the Hulme

Welcome to the club

Crescents[3] and working in Vinyl Exchange in Manchester city centre gave her a vital connection to the Manchester DJ community. She speaks confidently of DJ Michelle,[4] of starting at Flesh as a duo with her then partner Lin and of later DJ'ing at Paradise Factory with Phillipa Jarman.[5] During the early Flesh era, she cites Nadine, Paula and Tabs[6] as DJs who were also on the scene. To Kath, 'DJ'ing didn't feel unusual as there were a lot of really great women in Manchester and it felt like we were all coming through at the same time.' Happy as I am to share that more women came through in the early nineties, none were people of colour. It would be 2000 before Claud Cunningham and her Black Angel party and community arrived in Manchester to inspire the LGBTQIA+ scene.

Around the same time, Dulcie Danger remembers following a DJ in Brighton called Sarah Chapman: 'She was literally my idol,' she says. 'I'd go everywhere she was playing. I used to carry her record box. Every now and then she'd let me have a little go. She was pivotal in Brighton.' DJ Colleen 'Cosmo' Murphy studied sound and radio at NYU where Lynn McVey oversaw the radio station. She sponsored Colleen for a scholarship, kept an eye on her and would take her out to lunch. She was her only female mentor. Colleen also lists a post-1999 roll call of significant players including Jeannie Hopper (Liquid Sound Lounge) and Jennifer – who, alongside her, were the only women to play at François K and John Davis's Sunday session 'Body and Soul'.[7] Then there was Belinda the hip hop DJ, Jackie Christie[8] who played harder house and reigned supreme on the gay scene, and Chris Spirit (who played with Junior Vasquez). For Lakuti, 'honour goes to Judy at Fabric who was always really supportive'. None of whom feature enough in the history books that matter.

FAQs (female asked questions)

When Jamz became a specialist presenter at Reprezent radio, her mentor, Gavin Douglas – G-Child – encouraged her to learn how to DJ. He sold her his CDJs and made her mix live on air each week. She laughs – 'Even though I sounded awful and my knees would be knocking. I needed that kick up the arse – you know – be about it. Without that push from him I wouldn't have taken it seriously. He was very much tough love with me.' Her timeline jumps to Annie Mac's sell-out KOKO takeover in 2011, seeing this as the pivotal moment when a woman DJ blazed onto her radar. Prior to that, she says, her key influences had all been men: G-Charles, Ronnie Herel, Target and Trevor Nelson.

Although female DJ role models were hard to find, there was a little more diversity within the record labels themselves. Caroline Prothero recalls:

> At Virgin Records there was a woman, Jo McCormack, who signed the Spice Girls and then there was Cheryl Robson.[9] The Head of TV was a woman, and the Executive Vice President was Nancy Berry,[10] the fiercest woman in the music industry full stop. I became friends with her. I then had this really strong role model.

Ang Matthews (Manager at the Haçienda) enthuses:

> I remember having a conversation about it with Leroy [Richardson][11] – we thought, 'God, is this the only organisation that is neither sexist nor racist?' In the Factory offices there was Tracy Donnelly, Tina in legal, Seema Saini (receptionist / clerical); Lesley Gretton was at senior-management level, Teresa Allen was responsible for accounts; there was Suzanne Robinson in the kitchen. I'd landed in an environment that was really supportive of women.

One of the biggest influences and role models to us as DJs and record label executives was Strictly Rhythm's Gladys Pizarro, a five foot four, Latina lesbian and self-starter who, from 1989, took the world of independent record labels, branding, licensing and A&R to another level. Alongside her business partner, Mark Finkelstein, she launched the global careers and chart hits of some of the world's most celebrated and famous artists (mainly Black, Latino and Hispanic) including Roger Sanchez, Masters at Work, Armand Van Helden, Erick Morillo, India, Barbara Tucker and Ultra Nate.

Of starting Strictly Rhythm in 1989 Gladys says:

> This was all trial and error. We didn't have a book on this, I loved it. I was there seven days a week 365 days a year. It was my *Cheers*; that place where I felt most accepted, where I could be me.
>
> I made the tribe. I started working with Todd Terry; then he brought in Kenny Dope Gonzalez, Kenny brought in Louie Vega and it started to create a snowball effect. It was never just a business deal, it became a friendship, a family. I'm lucky that I still have relationships with practically everyone on that label and what's really special is that they are all still relevant.
>
> I'm a street kid and proud of it. The business of doing business out there, I brought that in here. Let's be real here. Let's break bread.

Community forged their relationships far better than the corporate machine.

Judy Griffith[12] recalls:

> I didn't really have any Black female role models growing up, apart from my mum, whom I worshipped. I was a massive vinyl junkie and Strictly Rhythm was a label I used to buy all the time. All my Strictly records had this woman's name on. This myth of a name. Gladys Pizarro. I saw this woman's name and that was enough for me to feel like I could work for a record company. Maybe I could be an A&R. I'd never seen A&R with any woman's name up until this point … For me to end up working at that same record label was – is this really happening for me? … If I hadn't worked at Strictly

FAQs (female asked questions)

> I could never have done Fabric and If I hadn't done two seasons in Ibiza meeting people and getting all those contacts I would never have been able to do that job with Strictly.

Gladys comments that when Strictly Rhythm started, people didn't get the Pizarro / Finkelstein dynamic. She says: '[In those days] finding women in the office was strange – how difficult it was to perceive that this woman was here for more than serving men, making the tea or typing invoices.' Unsurprisingly, we all know that feeling.

Throughout the nineties and noughties, native New Yorker and Maxi Records' owner Claudia Cuseta was my stateside inspiration, motivator, cheerleader and guardian angel. In an environment where women were considered either property or administrative cannon fodder and knowing nothing about the industry but being a 'House of Fields'[13] club kid, she rose through the ranks from Tommy Boy Records where she was inspired and worked alongside the mythical Monica Lynch (Vice President), at the New Music Seminar, and as the Club Promoter responsible for all the labels through Maurice Levy's Roulette Records. She then worked for Profile Records, which like Strictly Rhythm was a small label where everybody does everything. In 1990 she started Maxi Records with business partner Kevin McHugh who brought a fresh perspective and new contacts to the mix of her full understanding of where a record came from and how to get it through from concept to distribution and licensing. Maxi was a force to be reckoned with alongside Strictly Rhythm, Nervous and Tribal. By the power of word of mouth and some outsized mariachi shirts, Claudia and Kevin also notably introduced the party aspect to the Miami Winter Music Conference, holding a costume party at the Cama Drag in the first years when it moved from Fort Lauderdale to Miami Beach. Up until then the Winter Music

Conference had been a serious affair. Claudia cites her love of performance-art-heavy Danceteria and its resident DJ Anita Sarko as an inspiration. She says it was female DJs that she looked up to, and while there was a culture of parties using female DJs in New York, it wasn't really acknowledged, and it is not surprising that those women didn't get their due.

Over the years, females have become more visible, and progress has been made. Starting aged nineteen at 1Xtra,[14] Jamz Supernova says: 'All my bosses were Black women – Janine Kempadoo was my superior, then Ruby Mulraine; seeing these Black women in powerful positions I thought that was how it was until I ventured out of that floor into other areas of the BBC when I realised that it was a utopia. It's not like that at all anywhere else. In 2018–19 when Jaguar[15] applied for the BBC internship programme, she clicked instantly with 1Xtra's Sarah Jane Crawford who was really welcoming to her, then when she gained full time employment with Radio 1 *Introducing* she found it important to have strong mentors. She says:

> Annie Mac was always my hero. The first few times I met her I was so scared. I remember at Glastonbury 2019 – she was asking how I was and how the DJ'ing was going and she said – if you ever need any advice let's do some stuff in the studio. End of 2019, I did get in touch – then it was me, Annie [Mac], Clara [Amfo] and their producers in the studio. They asked me 'What do you want to achieve?' and gave me advice on how to do it. It was so generous of them to give me their time and support. I met Clara when I was an intern at 1Xtra; we kept in touch from then. She made me believe I could do it. There are people who make you feel like you can't. But because of the belief of others whom I respected, I could believe in myself.

Later, when Jaguar was chosen for the Smirnoff internship her mentor was The Blessed Madonna, of whom she says:

FAQs (female asked questions)

'I spent the day with Marea (TBM) ... she took us shopping at Phonica, then she invited me onto her Radio 1 residency live and that was a real turning point. She has been so great ever since.' Is it possible to navigate and evolve within the profession without such exceptional mirrors of affirmation of the divine feminine? Yes.

Lakuti says:

> The journey is always a little bit easier with company ... Earl Gateshead – he was around for a long time – he played in a bar in Chinatown in Soho; Ashley Beedle, Spencer from Goya music would hang there, his spot influenced a lot of people. He had a residency for twenty-five years where he played jazz, funk, soul. He took a liking to me, and he'd take me everywhere he went. He introduced me to all the broken-beat stars like IG Culture and Ade Fakile at Plastic People when it moved to Shoreditch. Earl was so integral to my story and he's the one that really connected the dots for me. He introduced me to the people at record stores. I was fortunate to have somebody so generous in my life to guide me and let me have a go with him in the studio.

Similarly, Cosmo recalls:

> I had two mentors who were helping me – David Mancuso and François Kervorkian but they weren't helping me commercially ... The Loft was failing, and the flyers didn't have my name on them. François was the one who first booked me for Body and Soul. Tommy Musto put my first record out on Suburban in 1998. I felt very supported in that way.

Chart-topping DJ / Producer Roger 'Wildchild' McKenzie and his partner Donna personally coached Dulcie in mixing and set building, while Kath McDermott and I are eternally grateful to Lucy Scher for her insistence on giving women an equal platform and without whom the female energy so vital to Flesh would have been non-existent.

Welcome to the club

Jamz Supernova interprets the importance of a strong mentoring relationship like this:

> Belief in you, when it is coming from someone who has already done it, says that you can get that far. That opens something inside of you. Seeing is believing. A mentor doesn't have to be someone you know or working in your field. It makes a massive difference. Mary Anne Hobbs and Gilles Peterson are my friends, but they probably don't realise they're my mentors. It doesn't matter if they aren't where you are, in the creative industry there is no logical step.

So, if DJ'ing isn't difficult for a woman to do and there's help available, why don't more women do it?

No one said it is easy. The stakes are high. Before you've opened your mouth or played a track, that feeling of being judged, imposter syndrome or having something to prove i.e. that you're not 'just a girl' or 'not bad for a woman' bristles the baby hairs on your neck. DJ'ing takes years of masochistic resilience, absolute dedication, meticulous preparation, exacting research, long-term investment, and unpaid graft. It is not a cash cow or an oven-ready career. Its nerdy, techy nature lacks the glamour and instant gratification that singing, modelling or Tik-Tokking offer. It requires a high level of competence and confidence in using technical equipment – you cannot be fazed by the technology, buttons, faders, cables, USBs, SD cards. DJ'ing requires performing regularly in front of different crowds to build a profile. This means securing regular bookings, networking, negotiating, presentation, long hours, DIY parties, building a following, and being seen to be working regularly enough to make that all important leap from part-time / weekend DJ to full-time, self-employed touring DJ. It means you have to take a leap of faith but remember to maintain your parachute. To join the big league you must demonstrate year-on-year progress; there has to be some kind of strategy or plan in motion. This can take years to establish.

Perhaps more women don't do it because the 'one in, one out' weapon of mass rejection is disheartening. Tokenism is a form of abuse that means that the one person who meets the selection criteria must then represent their race and gender for as long as they are employed there. The door opening shrinks to a funnel that slowly drip-feeds talent. And when the holding bay on the floor below becomes oversubscribed, many simply abandon their bags and leave. There's only so much waiting around you can do for that one prestigious vacancy that an entire workforce is in competition for. This is more pronounced for women of colour, for whom the glass ceiling in the higher / management levels is tempered and blacked out so we're less likely to try to break through it. The solution? Someone or something large must make way or step aside to make room for more than one appointment every ten years.

Many men apply for jobs knowing they meet only 60 per cent of the criteria, while women only apply for jobs when they know they meet 100 per cent of the criteria. This unconscious filter has its effect on the workforce at every level. Perfectionism is the enemy of equality: it stifles the pioneering spirit, suffocates the entrepreneurial mindset, and chokes creativity. With a little unlearning we can bypass these obstacles.

There wasn't a huge amount of supporting literature for anyone who followed DJ'ing as their vocation through the eighties and nineties. There weren't any instruction manuals, idiot's guides, 'how to' handbooks, nor were there accredited music business courses, or media internships that might jet propel your DJ progress. Today no career happens by accident. The new generation of DJs are fearless, focused, in control from the outset and benefit from the educational and vocational opportunities available. From The BRITS to BIMM, from Point Blank College to Future DJs, professional and academic coaching and extracurricular involvement is now a respectable path to follow.

Whether through pirate, community, local, university or online channels, most of us chose radio as our entry level introduction to a media career. When studying for an English degree at Leeds University, Jaguar indulged her passion for journalism and music by signing up for the student radio station. She was offered a Friday-night show, and from this was encouraged to apply for the internship programme at Radio 1 and 1Xtra, which she got. Of her time working across the early *Breakfast Show*, Sarah Jane Crawford's 1Xtra daytime show and Annie Mac's Friday show she says:

> This was two months paid working in radio production. I learned so much, it gave me a lot of confidence, which pushed me out of my comfort zone to learn how to speak to people, not be afraid to ask questions, send emails or reach out to people and it opened the door to the BBC for me which is where I am now.

The internship led first to a job with BBC *Introducing* in Sheffield in 2016; then she was offered a full-time position in London with the BBC *Introducing* Central Management team. This was when she started to grow and fully represent radio. At the same time Jaguar had a bug for working, so she applied for and got an Internship with *Mixmag*. This put her on another steep learning curve, which led her to becoming the Weekend Editor for the magazine website.

Of course, competition for BBC internships is fierce but there are many other avenues available. In London, Erica McKoy[16] was encouraged by a careers counsellor to apply to the Transmission Roundhouse Radio Station.[17] She was fifteen when she secured a weekly slot. Considering her experience she says:

> I'd go to these sessions at the Roundhouse where they'd teach me to make a radio show and I could feel my improvement progress every week. I remember I was so nervous – I went there by myself; others had come with their people. I wasn't a graduate and I wasn't eighteen ... It allowed me to get my first job at *Sky News* – then from *Sky News* I got jobs at the BBC.

Jamz Supernova followed the vocational route to the BRITS School where she relaxed into her identity and found her voice. She remembers the course fondly:

> At the BRITS school I did a two-year BTEC course. I did Media – radio, TV, photography, web design – written academic but very hands-on and I loved it. I'd come from school in Deptford where I felt like I was suppressing a big part of me and going to the BRITS school where everyone is uniquely themselves and has no care in the world about what people think meant I could be on that spectrum of quirky – I could just be me.

This is the kind of progress I love. More please.

There is a Pam Brown quote that says 'When sisters stand shoulder to shoulder, who stands a chance against us?' In Manchester, and in my more recent career, I've found this to be true, but it's not always been like this. Kim Benjamin (Cultural Creator, Founder of Kimco Entertainment) states:

> There was a time in my life when I felt like a lot of women were working against each other. And I just can't get behind that. I felt like it was simpler to be friends with guys ... I think there's a lot of stronger women now – there has been this shift where a lot more women feel empowered. I think before a lot of women just really hid. Life has changed – the music industry used to be like a ghost town of women. Claudia Cuseta was a rarity. Claudia, Kier[18] and I were alike. We were all pretty eccentric.

The question of sisterly solidarity is a familiar sticking point. Lakuti vents: 'Men support one another. There's a silent agreement that they will stick by one another no matter what. But the world shapes women and puts women in those competitive situations. We have to look beyond that and see the strength in coming together.' Continuing the theme of unity, Marcia Carr enthuses, 'Of course, I am going to look out for my sisters. I know – Black or white – we are still marginalised, side-lined, oppressed; we are still an afterthought. And I don't care if you are straight or a lesbian – I am going to support my sisters.' Cosmo expands this further, saying: 'I've always been a supporter of affirmative action for every underrepresented minority, just because until it's evened out that's what you have to do. It doesn't mean that you drop the standard; you still use the best.'

So how does this translate in real terms in the nightclub / events environment? Judy Griffith recounts the All Queens night at Fabric with Mary Anne Hobbs in 2022. She says: 'We had all female artists and all females working on the roles in the club. We don't want to always do these nights but if we need to shine a light on it we will.'

All cite a sense of responsibility to keeping the culture alive and vibrant. Jaguar refers me to an Audre Lorde quote: 'The human race is evolving through women.'

I think she is right. The music industry is a place where women create an extraordinary level of opportunity every day, so yes, it is our duty to help other women. In this we must lead by example. We must be open not threatened and invite people to learn from us and with us. Not only do we stand on the shoulders of our ancestors, but we can learn to dance balanced on the feet of our younger siblings. It benefits us all if we can learn to communicate, collaborate and integrate the experiences and lessons in both directions.

FAQs (female asked questions)

Being new to people after thirty years in the game is refreshing but also a bizarre intersection for me to have parked in. Why don't people know more about us? Lakuti comments:

> As an African Black queer woman I am tired of our story not being relevant and our contribution to music not being seen. I would like to hear more and see more of people like us being supported, being honoured, and playing a role in this industry should be normalised ... We need more Black editors and more Black writers who can tell the story in a sympathetic way.

For me, it's not just the Black writers that are needed. We need more female writers, female editors, female producers and commissioners to balance out the white, male, cis gatekeepers' gaze and editorial bias that controls what we see and hear on the TV, radio and in the music / dance magazines. We must also take control of our own narrative and tell our own stories. Some of the most interesting music biographies in recent years have been written by women – stories that are more valuable because they are not the predictable rock and roll stories.[19]

Frustrated by the erasure of women's contribution to DJ'ing, rave culture, electronic dance music and the fall-off in bookings and high-profile gigs for myself and many of my peers, I undertook a collaborative project with DJ / Producer Chris Massey (Sprechen Records), which gave us an opportunity to right this ship. I wrote some lyrics to Chris's demo, which I originally entitled 'I Like Girls'. It was to be a Grace Jones / Ian Dury-styled love letter to female DJs that made the argument about visibility and respect and offered a clap back to Daft Punk and Soulwax's 'Teachers' where, in fifty or so name checks, not one female DJ or producer was credited to have influenced their work. The song was quickly retitled 'Sheroes'.

Welcome to the club

We completed it in just under a year, with some fifteen rewrites, four home-studio recording sessions plus two considerable studio edits cutting it down from a ten-minute opus to a six-minute odyssey. We knew we would be criticised for excluding people (some were originally featured but had been edited out). We did not anticipate an accusation of plagiarism: proving our originality in private while the public social media court was in session took some shine off our good intention. Situation calmed, Chris first pitched it to the female-run labels but had no takers. 'Sheroes' was signed to Black Riot Records and released in 2018, coinciding with the centenary of the Suffragette movement.

Paradoxically, it was a collaboration with a male DJ and producer, a male mix engineer, mastering by HiFi Sean, a trio of male remixers, Seb: our male videographer, Brett: our male supporting artist in the video, and a record label run by two men that helped me to release a record about fiercely independent and kickass women. The feminine energy entered when Nemone and The Blessed Madonna supported it on BBC 6 Music.

Somehow history doesn't favour women or women's stories. No matter how many plates we spin, or how many awards we win, our contribution is credited to the man with the cheque book or who's sitting nearest to our seat, or it's overlooked, its significance undermined. In life and in the media, successful women are liked less than successful men – fact. If we achieve, it is rumoured that we've slept or manipulated our way to it while men earn their accolades fair and square (even when a woman is known to have been behind their success). It's maddening that this still happens. All the women I interviewed reported situations in the boardroom where they have been passed over, talked over, ignored or shouted down. Some say that, post-pandemic, they must shout louder to maintain the authority and visibility that has been broken by Google Meet, Zoom meetings and working from home. The habit of not speaking up, of being content operating in the background while letting others shine in the spotlight complicates this. But things are changing.

Judy Griffith says:

> I don't think peers and people around me realise what an impact George Floyd and #blm made. It wasn't just about what happened: it has given me and lot of my colleagues of colour a lot more confidence and more of a voice. Before I might not have elaborated on some things. Now I'm becoming more confident to speak up about certain things – even in interviews. I feel most of my time I remain invisible. The amount of people that have said, 'What I had no idea there was a woman behind Fabric.' I realise that that's because I never pushed myself – we always had Craig Richards as the ambassador, and I was always happy to take that position but now I am sad about that.

The level of scrutiny over personal relationships is something that male DJs never face. As a woman, I've found that DJ'ing and starting a relationship, the 'who' plus all the changes and all the challenges that accompany it, occupy more bandwidth than they should. While, at the other end of the scale, ageing and menopause bookend our biological and professional retirement. Of these, the varied experiences of pregnancy, motherhood and getting back behind those decks draws the most unwelcome attention and results.

Marcia Carr's daughter Malaika was born in 1992 and the rearing and childcare fell largely to her. Of this time, she says:

> It was a career stumbling block because problems with childcare meant I had to turn down bookings. Her father wasn't stable or present in her life and I was a bit proud, would

Welcome to the club

> not ask for help. I had to turn down a lot of work for many years as I was now responsible for this small person. That was humbling and disheartening. Malaika came with me to record shops when I started back out – or she would come with me to the *Touch Magazine* offices. I wasn't going to sit in my house for ten years.

No matter how far we've evolved, women instinctively shoulder the responsibility to nurture, care and tend to our families, prioritising this over career. While working we carry ourselves simultaneously through several of life's benchmark idiosyncrasies that men never need consider. There is no provision and no rule book for this and working through it in the public eye can be hard. Pregnancy and / or menopause is every woman's Room 101.

Kath McDermott worked monthly until she was eight months pregnant. After she had her daughter she got myalgic encephalomyelitis[20] and found herself bedbound and housebound for a long time. She knew she was getting ill because she found it difficult to listen to music. She was reconnected slowly to music years later by Rina Ladybeige at Social Services, who invited her to play as she had inspired her so much. Then Matthew Rothery at 'Kiss Me Again' and she found that she could slot straight back in. Self-care and self-awareness were the key to her return.

On leaving Radio 1 Annie Mac's final tweet concluded:

> In my time at Radio 1, I have fallen in and out of love, moved homes, climbed up the career ladder, got married and become a mother twice over, alongside your doing versions of the same. Thank you for allowing me into your lives. Thank you for brightening my days.

The BBC *Newsbeat* supporting article, headlined 'Legend: Annie Mac is leaving BBC1 after 17 years',[21] quotes Annie's Instagram post, writing: 'The Irish DJ said on Instagram:

FAQs (female asked questions)

'I need more time to see my kids in the evenings now they are both in school. I would like more time to write fiction and to create podcasts.' All of which she has done and created a club night for ravers who want to be home before midnight.

One of London's most successful midweek events through the late nineties and noughties was 'Missdemeanours'. It was, as Caroline terms it, 'the original social network', where industry heads and creatives gathered every Thursday to listen to music, make deals and party hard. Organised by PRO Director Caroline Prothero and DJ Lottie[22] – the Missdemeanours party ended when Lottie got married, had a baby and her outlook on life, work and parental responsibilities changed.

Colleen met a myriad of obstacles when her daughter Ariana was born in 2004. She says that she hit the glass ceiling when she had a baby and remarks:

> everything changes anyway but when you get pregnant there's no support. There is also a physicality to it that people block. One guy in Poland tried to cancel me because I was pregnant. A booking agent dropped me for the same reason. I couldn't get an agent: if they already had a woman on the roster, they wouldn't take me. I ended up making a lot of music during that time …
>
> People kind of forgot about me. I'd brought all these guys up but there was no two way … Rights for women have changed substantially in the last thirty years. I think if I got pregnant now, I would have a bigger career.

My ultimate working mother is personified by Jamz Supernova, a devoted mum, a tireless polymath presenting on radio, TV, fronting awards ceremonies and documentaries, DJ'ing in clubs, running a record label and producing a podcast. She is visible on social media but not obsessively so. When I comment on her sweet Instagram posts of three-month old Forrest in the hot seat behind the desk at 6 Music, she says candidly:

When I was on maternity leave – when there was no radio, no DJ gigs, just me looking after her, I was still looking for music. You have to stay current. I was still watching documentaries because I love it.' She prioritises family first saying, "Forrest comes before all of that. Even saying to my manager, 'I'm not contactable or online at these hours." When I say no to an opportunity, I don't feel like I've missed anything ... But me going back to work isn't just financial. I do it because I love it.

Even with this progressive attitude to motherhood, Jamz still felt anxious about being considered 'just a mum' or being side-lined at work. A shift in perspective helped: 'Yeah so what if I am a mum? You have to lean into that ... You have to think "so what". If you don't think like that it's not just the end for you, it's the end for everybody.'

It is an uncomfortable truth that women (DJs) with children do struggle and there is no real support. In November 2022 Ofsted reported that amidst rising costs parents struggle to find childcare in the UK at a price that they can afford.[23] When mothers leave their jobs to have children the money they lose is substantial and when they go back to work, most find that their salary only covers the costs of childcare. DJ contracts and fees do not have built-in crèche or childcare buyouts, events rarely make provision for parenting on site, while timing feeds, changes and sleeps can make travelling and set times unfeasible.

If motherhood wasn't tricky enough, as we mature, we find that we can bounce out of editorial favour, while our interview questions become less about legacy and more about retirement. Damn those optics.

Marcia Carr wrote in a Facebook status update 22 July: 'Apparently thirty-seven years of hard work means nothing to some people in this fickle industry. I "am not hip" because I am not on certain agents' books, I do not look a

FAQs (female asked questions)

certain way, and don't do PC trends. Thank God I know my worth.'

Men never have to think that what they look like might affect the bookings they get whereas for women this is everyone's prime concern. Why should being an older woman deny you the right to DJ – why doesn't age affect men in the same way? When voted 'Woman of the Year' at the Billboard Women In Music Awards in 2016,[24] Madonna said: 'I think the most controversial thing I have ever done is to stick around.' It's clear that women in music, media and the arts are date and time stamped while men aren't. A recent *New York Times* article on Honey Dijon[25] reads: 'Dijon likes to say that she was born in Chicago but grew up in New York, where she moved in the late nineties. (She does not, however, like to say her age, calling the question "really sexist and horribly boring".).' Lakuti takes this up:

> You never hear a man mention their age as a DJ. With guys these things never come into play. As a woman everything is framed around your age. This is IMMEDIATE which is fascinating for the so-called circles we are in that are meant to be progressive. You don't get gendered when you're a guy but when you are a woman they make it clear. Apart from the legacy she's leaving behind. Isn't that the highlight? But no 'thank you for your services'. This thing will only change when the men stand up to say – I'm 55 or 60 and it's not relevant … I know a lot of DJs that are much older than me but nobody ever really knows their age.

Journalist and academic, Kamila Rymajdo found that some women are not keen to discuss their careers in terms of gender.

> They hide behind 'I don't see myself as a female DJ' or do not want to be put in that box of the one who keeps banging on about it and I can see that. But the issue is the gender

> disparity in pay. Despite the days of the man earning the family wage being long since passed, salaries for the top artist / senior management positions are almost exclusively male and fees are still male-weighted. When we look at the top 10 DJs – we find that they are all male, and when we google top-earning female DJs, even the women we would consider to be on an equal footing haven't dipped a toe into the Forbes top 30. The opportunities are there but when we get there the balance sheets don't reflect this. Why is this? Because as women we are not encouraged to know our worth, to discuss this openly in financial terms and / or ask for what we want whereas men do this instinctively and it is respected ... the fact that you can't advance, that once you hit forty you can't go further. A lot of the younger DJs just didn't want to talk about that because it doesn't affect them yet and there's been a turn against feminism that meant it wasn't important to them to pursue that angle. Later on there was push back – people don't want to be characterised as 'old'. Ageing is taboo and ageism is something we have all internalised. People don't want their age to be out there so will deny experiencing it. It's like admitting some kind of weakness.[26]

When I shared her official *Resident Advisor* article on ageism[27] as a story on my Instagram page, it attracted a pile-on of negative / sarcastic commentary from young, white female DJs mainly under thirty who felt that the content 'was shit' and did not apply to them. The negativity was so bad I had to have the post removed. Maybe they'll understand it when they're older.

When Annie Mac left Radio 1 in 2021 it marked the end of a seventeen-year tenure at the top of her broadcasting game. Discussing her departure, she is quoted as saying: 'that she does not take her position in an industry still dominated by men for granted, aware that, at her age, many women in music are ignored, sidelined, or just "invisible".' Warming to the theme, she says: 'But there's just something about the spirits of women in their middle age that is quite incredible.'[28]

Maybe it's because when we hit middle age we care more about the issues, the politics and who is coming up behind us and we care less about the superficiality and what people think about us. When I weighed it up, I felt I had nothing to lose and everything to gain from going public about all of it. DJs Nikki Beatnik, Anja Schneider, Sarah Sweeney and BB Supernature have each publicly addressed ageism in the electronic music industry in the press and social media, while Kamila Rymajdo's article in *Resident Advisor* and her chapter in the book *The Evolution of Electronic Dance Music* go some way towards breaking the taboo. It's frustrating that women would rather ignore the issue than let this vulnerability show. Getting old simply means you're thankfully and happily alive.

Having lost many young friends to illness and suicide, I'm grateful for every day of my life and proud of my age. Leaning into this has been liberating; once the truth is out there's nothing to be afraid of. I think this is what Annie Mac meant about that middle-aged spirit. It's powerful and self-assured. At fifty-three, Colleen says she's happy seeing her career peak. She is doing the best work she's ever done, adding that there is something to be said for slow and steady, for having more maturity and experience and knowing better how to deal with things. I will celebrate the day with balloons and cake when I see our maturity shining out from the cover of dance-music magazines. Legacy and heritage means having older women on the cover too.

Learning, respect and appreciation is a two-way street. Lakuti suggests that intergenerational collaboration will push this forward. She says:

Welcome to the club

> I would hope that older people stop looking at young people with scepticism and start putting themselves out there, interacting with younger people. Without young people pushing me and supporting me I wouldn't be where I am today because when I started playing, it was young people bringing me into the show. The old established dudes did nothing for me. It was kids who were pushing me all the time. I appreciate them and like to listen to them and try to put myself on the same level. But not coming from the perspective that 'I am the great teacher I know it all and learn from me'. There needs to be mutual respect and coming together with a different attitude. A lot of the older people can be very negative and bitter on social media and this I feel is not the way of embracing young people.

There is an anonymous quote that runs: 'Behind every successful woman is a tribe of other successful women who have her back.' This is my dream for the future. If behind every successful man is a strong woman, there is no reason why we cannot divert those efforts to ourselves. Soon (I hope) all interviews will be equal, based on ability, talent, merit and music more than gender, optics, biology and chronology, but until they are, we can afford to be brave, be potent, be outspoken, be at peace with our imperfections, and if that fails to charm, then refuse to answer dumb questions. If a journalist dares to ask sexist, loaded questions then maybe it's time that we are better informed and devise some clever answers.

Like Maya Angelou says: 'Each time a woman stands up for herself, without knowing it possibly, without claiming it, she stands up for all women.'

5
How to kill a DJ

It's a crisp autumn evening in West London, the kind that takes your breath away as you talk. I'm walking home from dinner with a friend and whingeing about work, as saturnine Capricorns have a habit of doing. Suddenly it wasn't enough to be a talented DJ or presenter. Thanks to the tabloids, celebrity gossip columns and 'ladmags' a new kind of woman was being fetishised. 'Ladettes' or 'geezerbirds' were brash, gauche, unafraid of getting publicly and unapologetically wasted, matching the boys drink for drink, line for line, afterparty for afterparty, then facing the paparazzi off with some outrageous behaviour before going to work on children's / daytime TV or national radio. Celebrities like Lisa I'Anson, Kate Moss, Sienna Miller, Sadie Frost, Denise Van Outen (flashing her bra at Prince Charles while he was talking to Steps at Party in The Park), Zoe Ball, Sara Cox and Gail Porter (who was projected nude onto the Houses of Parliament by *FHM*) set the standard and hit gender politics like a wrecking ball.

The tide was turning for DJs too. Those who were dressed in designer gear, connected to a thrilling club, media, music or fashion circle, were hard-partying, younger and with the increasing prevalence of cocaine, ketamine and MDMA on one side and the Internet on the other, had begun to top the polls. Dance music was suddenly being marketed to men. The women had a new way of presenting their talent and it wasn't a behaviour that I could fake. Despite exposure with Channel 4's *Miami Nice*, *4Music* and guest presenting on TV, I'd failed to catch the next wave. Still only in my thirties, I no longer ticked any of the boxes required to advance. I was free-falling without anything or anyone to stop it.

As we rounded the stark brutalism of Erno Goldfinger's Trellick Tower, my friend, grizzled by my mood snarked: 'You know what your problem is, you're just not famous anymore.' It was a savage blow, but true – my fame flame had gone out.

Nothing prepares you for your 'ninety-nine no's and one maybe' moments. I didn't understand it nor did I know how to control it. Industry favours winners and because of this people are terrified of losing favour or flavour. The margin for error is slim, while any loss of status is a lingering odour that people will cross the street to avoid. Everybody knows but nobody talks about it, and nobody talks about you. The phone stops ringing. The silence is deafening. Your friendship circle becomes smaller; your social life less social. The psychological damage of defining yourself by your job kicks in. Then when everything stops spinning, you lose your balance and your sense of self.

As Todd Edwards says,

> No one talks about what it takes to generate a second wave of success once the first has gone. You can even be Kanye West and when you lose your throne for a moment you just can't handle it ... I know what it's like to have bottomed out ... But then I've been rescued and that's something to be thankful for.[1]

There was a chink in the clouds in 2001 when the Ministry of Sound launched their bespoke Internet radio station.

How to kill a DJ

Headed by David Dunne, Mark Ovenden and Gavin Kingsley, it had a short-term FM license then was available on DAB and online. My two-hour show, 'Hard and Soul', was live, with guests mixing and being interviewed in the studio. There were merchandise and CD competitions won by super-fan Demetrius Williams and a bunch of regular listeners around the world. While record labels didn't take anything online seriously until 1Xtra launched in 2002, I took it seriously, circulating my weekly playlists and feedback. I kept busy DJ'ing with regular spots at Rulin' and Tribalism at the Ministry of Sound, Vertigo at The Cross, Discotec at The End, and I continued to tour overseas.

I don't know how I'd have reacted if anyone had told me that DJ death is cyclical. It might have soothed me to know that I would soon find a way to climb out of the hole that I was in. I think I would also have liked to know that, like Groundhog Day, the hole would suck me in again. Had I known, I might have planned smarter instead of taking the spoils from the sale of my apartment and running like a bug-eyed raver straight into the disco lights of Paris. The time seemed right to make a fresh start and thankfully the move and the next eight years were ridiculously successful. Good job too, as by plugging myself into a different territory, I took myself off the UK market without realising it.

Had anyone advised me on how to handle this career crisis or an international move, the outcome could have been different, but nobody did and I didn't ask for help. It's sad that like so many similar experiences – ageism, sexism, racism and homophobia – we pretend that it isn't happening or that it doesn't exist. Losing your mojo is in the top 3 reasons for DJs giving in and hanging up their headphones.

Years later, an agent, a booker, a promoter and a DJ meet in an Amsterdam bar. This sounds like a joke but it's not.

Welcome to the club

Towards the end of their after-dinner conversation one of the three men says: 'You know, Paulette, no club will ever book a Black, female DJ with grey hair.' At this, the other two men laughed loudly. Preceding my big move to Ibiza by three months, their timing couldn't have been worse. I'd terminated my contract on my apartment and resigned from my agent, radio station and residency. There was no turning back.

I struggled through two barren years in Ibiza and started to wonder if their analysis was correct. I didn't have to wait long for confirmation. It was at the Glitterbox closing (September 2015), one of the last parties at Space Ibiza. Todd Terry had dropped Funky Green Dogs, 'Fired Up', as his last tune and I was dancing next to Martin, our master of ceremonies, the straight-talking Tracey (who was serving classic chic in a neutral silk Armani dress) and the fabulous Foxy (our debutante drag-glamourpuss). We were serving VIP fierceness.

'Can I say one thing ...' the authority in Tracey's voice cuts through loud music like a hot wire through ice, so I pay attention. She lowers her voice and continues, 'If I have one message for you it's ... nine months and go out laughing.' Such a curious prophesy to deliver on the dancefloor but when the Yoda visions come, share them she must. She explained over the music that I wasn't doing myself any favours playing nine-hour sets for a pittance in hotels, bars and restaurants where no one was listening. She could see that I was a good DJ but my appearances were too few, underpaid and insignificant. She said I was worth more than this and should seriously think about leaving. Her words landed with the boom of the confetti that fell to the dance floor, shot to pieces by the CO_2 cannons and the 'oohs' and 'aahs' of a startled crowd. I slid back to the beginning of the game. History repeats until we learn the lessons.

Starting over is terrifying and exciting. Doing it multiple times in different cities or other countries adds tension. It's turning to a new page full of possibility and fear. It's sitting in darkness until the light creeps in. It's finding new colours to add lustre to it all. It's the realisation that you've lost everything but you're alive and healing. It's grieving for the loss of a dream and a life and career you didn't succeed in manifesting.

It's my birthday when I return to Manchester, so I'm planning and thinking escape hatches and rescue remedies. I write on a Post-It 'The bigger the risk, the bigger the win' and on another 'It's not like I haven't been here before'. In my head, I triage the positive, useful lessons I've learned on Fantasy Island and let the negative ones go. This time I'm facing change head on. No more running. No more sitting at a table with a plate but never being allowed to eat. I'm saying 'no' to the toxicity of promoters, hotel and bar owners who bounce me like a 'not today / not for us' superball between themselves.

After Christmas I realise that I have no contacts, no work, no money and no idea how I'm going to survive the bitter Manchester winter in my gauzy Ibiza clothes, but I make a five-year plan and join a gym to show willing. After all, patience is one of my strong points. I'm hot-wired to idle in the holding zones between disaster, resurrection, redemption, recognition and transformation but for now I'm burnt out and need a break. Moving into my mother's house full-time as her primary carer meant that rest was not possible. I and my family entered a two-year phase of intensive care emergencies from January 2016. My five-year plan thus became a Tipp-Exed out, anything could happen, one day at a time, seven-year plan.

Killing a DJ does not require the employment of an expensive hitman. Keyboard warriors can achieve it with an itchy send finger, aided by the ensuing social media circus and cancel culture. Misbehaving like peak MTV or Instagram Kanye, Will Smith at the Oscars or Ten Walls on Facebook means that your demise is quick, public, painful and practically irredeemable. For the rest of us, time, systemic bias, racism, unfavourable editorial agendas, discrimination, bad planning, bad management, and some spectacularly bad decision-making are the 'choose one or all of the above' ingredients for disaster.

The quickest way to dodge these kinds of bullets in the music industry is to disappear and there are many invisibility cloaks available to you. A name change can be useful when you need to distance yourself from an imperfection that's spoiling an otherwise pristine legacy. It's a brave, 'kill or cure' move, but when done for the right reasons and handled sensitively it can be liberating. In 2020 The Black Madonna became Blessed and abundance poured forth on her head. That same year, Joey Negro metamorphosed into Dave Lee and there was no need for a St Louis-style funeral – life went on. But disappearing is not always helpful, constructive or productive. In a world where technology is evolving exponentially and we are transitioning from the Internet to the metaverse, having no online presence can seriously damage your health.

Having witnessed how easily audiences around the world could be simultaneously engaged through my weekly online show on Ministry of Sound radio, I commissioned my first website from Castrocorp[2] in October 2001. Designed originally in Flash, it was a symphony in black and red that despite taking ages to upload mixes and photos (thank you dial-up), was essential to maintaining 24/7 visibility without placing regular adverts in expensive magazines. In the last twenty-one years my site has undergone four redesigns, been hosted on servers in three countries and can now be found on www.djpaulette.co.uk, where it is faster, sleeker, smoother and contains the latest music, news, photos, videos and links to all social media platforms.

My family, friends and colleagues did not understand the first website, or see the importance of my posting regular blogs along with flyers, short iMovies and galleries of photos from each event. When Myspace launched nearly two years later in February 2003 the world got the memo. Hot @myspacetom[3] (everybody's first friend) and Myspace became a hotbed of discovery and a ticket sales / A&R and artists' dream. It became the most used platform in the world where anyone could post photos, blogs, flyers, posters, music and video clips. It was the genesis of Internet superstars and it was a gamechanger. WordPress also launched in 2003, making blogging easier. Then Facebook launched to the public in 2006 and by 2010 it had taken over the world, making Myspace obsolete. It all happened so quickly, there was an explosion of apps[4] and there was much confusion. It was a while before we realised that each platform had a different allure and market and that we could / should use all of them – not just one.

When Facebook developed fan pages for artists in 2007 I didn't see the point in duplicating pages and content so I invited a group of trusted super-fans to create and then take charge of the page. This backfired in 2009 when I asked to take control of the page to keep it more up to date. The disgruntled French fans blocked me, refusing to give me administrative control of the page or access to its community. I had to start another page but the loss of the community was damaging in virtual and real terms.

By 2015, when I moved back to the UK, the top five social media platforms – Facebook, Twitter, Instagram, YouTube and Snapchat – were all in regular daily use, with billions of accounts. They had become vital business tools and were now a pre-requisite for artist marketing in the music industry.

When people ask how I have managed to sustain my career and remain relevant, online presence is my answer. In 2022 it has become a benchmark for everyone, from artist agents to human-resources departments, on a global scale. Visibility is the key to sustainability and your social media presence tells people everything they need to know about you without them having to hire a private detective.

We obscure our own histories by simply not appearing in search-engine lists. The humble brag that 'I don't do social media' indicates immediately how far an artist or employee is willing to or can be projected to go. While artists like Anz and Josey Rebelle have deleted certain of their social media pages and have a permanent 'OOO' on their email accounts, they are omni-present online – Rinse FM, NTS, Bandcamp, Ninja Tunes, Fabric, *Resident Advisor*, Spotify, iTunes, Soundcloud, Mixcloud, Stamp The Wax, Beatport etc. all provide links back to them.

I don't TikTok, Snapchat or Twitch (never say never) but as a Black artist in a majority white environment, I know how important it is to keep one's profile high. The algorithms for viewing Black accounts are less favourable so if you don't engage on any social media platform you will struggle to be seen or heard. Putting yourself out there regularly in a shop window of your own creation is taking control of your history, your legacy and your archive. Yes, it's a humungous time-sponge and can be a lucrative, full-time job for many. But there is good reason why every organisation worth its sales projections has a website and a social media department or agency. Do not despair. If social media isn't for you, take a leaf out of Jamz Supernova's book. She says:

> I've taken on a team to handle my social media – it's expensive but if I pay someone to do it at least it is getting done. I send content and send a caption and they can put it out. Some people enjoy it and love being on social media, and that's amazing but I don't, and it has a big knock on my mental health.

Choices? Employ an agency to do this and make your life easier, or own your story, choose your platform and do it yourself. Unless you're an AAA-lister, being an online ghost scares journalists, editors, producers, agents, events organisers, employers and prospective partners.

How can we ensure that our place is secured in the archives that we can't control?

Prior to the Internet, Ceefax (and later Oracle and Prestel) was the earliest mass-digital information storage interface in use in Britain. It was initially created to provide televisual subtitles for deaf people but eventually became the first stop for information on news, sport, weather, entertainment, television and radio listings and businesses. It was often the first to report a breaking news story or headline[5] and the tortoise-slow page updates brought us cheap holidays and flights. Aside from this, archival information from newspaper, journal and magazine sources were bound together in volumes, photos were stored on sheets of plastic slides, contact sheets went into envelopes and all hard copies were stored in massive boxes on shelves, in filing cabinets in dusty rooms or in the endangered species now known as a library. If issues were damaged or missing the volumes were incomplete. As the popularity of the Internet rose, we realised we could store more information in less space and access it faster on computer. At the end of the nineties there was a scrabble to scan in and digitise all existing material. Decisions had to be made about how far back records were to be registered and some information didn't make the cut. Daniel Newman's cute picture of me sitting on the life-sized polar bear in Tutu Tedder's back garden for *DJ Mag* in 1994? Lost to the ether. If, like mine, your best feature or photo fell foul of a cut-off date, then the chances are that your info-trail will be smaller than it should.

Another time was 1998. To those who made contributions to the scene that haven't been recognised, I salute you. Back then we were just doing our jobs. The scene itself was still in its infancy and hadn't gathered the almighty head of steam it has now. So that DJ in Scotland, that annual street party in France or dingy club in Bolton did not get the coverage that hindsight now realises it should have. But I see you.

Now how's this for an observation? 'History is written by the winners – the winners in dance music have mainly been men. Men are more likely to push themselves forward and take the credit.' Carl Loben.

Most books on DJs, electronic music, rave and the music industry have been written by men. And despite there being many important and celebrated female artists and female journalists, editors and authors[6] from the nineties to the present day, the pattern persists. White cis males are the trusted gatekeepers commissioned to report on, document and dissect the scene.[7] Their articles, features and books have become recognised and revered as the truth, the whole truth and nothing but the truth. They have become the standard by which all other books must be judged even though some of the information is missing. I took some of the gatekeepers to task and this is what I discovered.

Peter Hook's book *The Haçienda: How Not to Run a Club* (2009) took three years to write, has never been out of print, has had no revisions and has sold in excess of 500,000 copies. I have sometimes felt left out, so I asked Peter if he thought his story was the whole truth. He replied:

> If somebody writes a book it is their responsibility, and their memory. Don't forget ever that it's your truth. Each one of us would have a completely different memory. This is going to be, has to be my story, my escapades. You have to be true to yourself ... I have been left out of many things I shouldn't have, in my opinion of course, and I like you will always be there, because we made the story and always will.

This gave me such a boost. I didn't expect to walk away from that Zoom feeling two foot taller, but I did.

Last Night a DJ Saved My Life, written by Bill Brewster and Frank Broughton (Headline, 1999) was the first book to trace a complete history of DJ'ing. It charted at no. 45 in the *Observer Monthly* and was quoted as 'one of the greatest music books'.[8] Their original submission was intended to cover the period of disco from Stonewall 69 up to the Aids Crisis in 1983 – but it was Frank's university friend, Doug Young's,[9] brainwave for them to expand it to cover the complete history of DJ'ing because no one had done it with that kind of scope or from a transatlantic perspective before. There have now been two revisions, the latest published by White Rabbit Books in 2022, which I was invited to interview for. I'm curious to know why it was time to refresh their browser.

Bill and Frank made the decision to update it, firstly to get it back into print and make it readable to a new and younger audience. Their intention was that twenty-five-year-olds should be able to pick it up and not feel like it was written twenty years ago. In the original book, Bill and Frank were focused on tracing the evolution of the craft and the skills, so women were side-lined because their stories weren't in that line of transmission. Details about the acid house years were also left out because Sheryl Garratt was publishing her book[10] around the same time and was focused directly on that culture. The techno content had proved hard to lock down because they couldn't get any interviews with the major players. It was only with the second version of *Last Night* that they interviewed Kevin Saunderson and Derrick May but still couldn't get an interview with Juan Atkins. Documenting the whole truth is a tricky and ongoing process.

Bill Brewster underpins this:

> The book (LNADJSML) is 250,000 words long and, although that's a lot of words, if you break it down into all the people it covers, it's really not very much. Outside of the big obvious protagonists (Kool Herc, Francis Grasso, David Mancuso, Frankie Knuckles, Larry Levan), most of the characters in the book might only get a few mentions or even one.
>
> I really don't see these as sleights on someone or a comment that the rest of their career is not worthy of mention, it's just that there is a bigger story that we are telling which is that of The DJ and what he or she did next.
>
> I've done 10,000-word interviews and only included a 100-word quote, but the details in each interview are vital in understanding what happened at a particular time and being able to document it as accurately as we can.

While *Welcome to the club* is about exhuming the hidden histories, I've had to hide a few bodies myself. The writing process was the culprit. When the time came, some people were too busy, unavailable or had too many commitments. It was hard to leave Smokin Jo out as she's such an important and integral part to the story, but since she was writing her book and asked to withdraw, I had to respect that. Chasing people was a drain: I suppose you can invite a guest to Zoom but you can't make them think. I understand that 'omission' or 'being overlooked', that source of professional paranoia and mistrust, isn't always down to a writer's malicious intent. There is often no agenda other than time or space running out. Writing to deadlines means that you must be flexible and prepared to sculpt your content around the strongest stories in your narrative arc. Those that don't fully materialise, we paraphrase around and those who decline, we forget. This means that once the book is published their history is eroded.

When asked how far he thinks their book has course corrected Frank asserts:

> I'm proud to say we didn't have to change much but we were really careful with the language. We demasculinised a lot of the language: we write 'the DJ' not 'he' or 'him'. It's subtle grammar changes like that that make the difference as it's all unconscious. We were very conscious about finding more quotes from women: we increased the number of female voices in the book … which makes it a better book and more rounded.
>
> The Jimmy Savile issue was an interesting thing that we changed – we confronted him head on. Rather than it being dismissed with a 'by the way' we said … he probably wasn't the first but here is the theme of a man abusing his DJ power. You have to acknowledge that everyone has a different relationship to him now which changes the way you can tell that story.
>
> Hilary Mantel writes, 'All history is fiction in some respect because we'll never know.' This is the third time we've updated the book – each time it becomes truer. Each time we get further away from that central line, and we bring more characters in. Each time we've updated and expanded it, it's become truer because some of those stories are women's … There were names that were in the original book that we hadn't followed up on like The Saint DJs – then we realised that Sharon White has an incredible story. She was the first DJ to play at Saint and the only female DJ to play at The Paradise Garage.

Welcome to the club

Sigh. It's fair to say that you need a titanium rod to stake your place in the history books. It's not just about who you are or what you've done, it's about how and when you do it, who sees the value in it, and how many record it for posterity. If you can stir up enough media support with photographers / journalists / editors / magazines / TV / radio your story will attain total audio-visual recall. Even if your contribution is clear or you win big, DJs from minorities, women (especially those who don't fit with the editorial style or agenda), those who are anxious or reserved when speaking to journalists or monosyllabic on radio shows can be easily dismissed. When editors make their decision it seems there's not much room for women.

You can also be overlooked when you stand in the shadow of giants. Carl Loben sets the record straight saying:

> Lisa Loud, Nancy Noise and Trevor Fung are arguably as important to the fabled tale of four young guys going to Ibiza and bringing acid house back to the UK. It is all so wide of the mark, ignoring the Haçienda in Manchester and what happened in Blackburn ... Fortunately for them [Oakenfold, Rampling et al.] they had a lot of music writers and photographers documenting what they did so more than anything else they had the media on their side.

Media relations are not always a fine bromance either. Carl remembers an ugly situation at *Melody Maker*: 'It was 1997 – the week after Roni Size and Reprazent had won the Mercury Music Prize – me and Neil Kulkarni had both suggested putting Roni Size on the cover but the Editor, Mark Sutherland, said, 'No – if we have a Black face on the cover, it doesn't sell magazines.' Somebody better tell those award-winning artists that their names weren't on the list.

The only way to stop these serial history killers is by publicly debunking and stopping celebrating the false past where women and minorities don't contribute to or exist in culture or society. It's time to provide a balanced commentary and celebrate the beauty of a diverse and inclusive present. We can do this. To this, Dave Haslam says:

> Obviously you'd hope that the industry you're a part of would be more enlightened, but it's just become a reflection of the world we live in. Cultural activity is being appropriated, muted, sold off. Women are never mentioned in the same breath as men. What can we do about changing that systemic thing in society? It requires a huge cultural revolution.

When George Floyd was murdered it sent seismic shockwaves around the world. Everyone with a social media account or online news service saw at first hand the brutal treatment he received. Black Lives Matter demonstrations were happening daily and suddenly everybody, every organisation, magazine, broadcaster, TV and news service, and advertiser had to assess and reposition themselves in terms of diversity, inclusion and equality.

DJ Magazine and *Mixmag* created two revelatory, groundbreaking magazine events that will stand as an incriminating reflection of our times and celebration of the Black electronic music culture for years to come with their Dance Music Is Black Music and Blackout issues. Both tackled the hidden histories question head on, examined genres that have been overlooked, and published heritage articles on artists, singers, producers and DJs that, with or without the bespoke issue, more than merit the attention.

When Jaguar called me to talk about *Mixmag*'s Blackout issue we were in lockdown. The issue was being steered by the producer Funk Butcher and it was to contain the people at the forefront of the scene and the pioneering voices that should be heard but don't often get the platform. I ranted to her for a good hour as I was cooking my dinner.

Mixmag was off-print but online so there would be no hard copy. The article I was being considered for included Stacy Hotwax, Sharon White and Smokin Jo. Jaguar said: 'I would have loved to have spoken to K-Hand and it's very special that I met Aunty P. Even Mista Jam said, "I've never heard of half of these women." It's the piece that I've written that I feel the most proud of. I learned a lot from all of you and I'm really glad I did it.'[11]

Jaguar states:

> #blm ... was a heavy time – I remember Blackout Tuesday – I have mixed feelings about it. I'd already planned my show that week – but I remade it and did an all-Black show with a statement at the beginning. Why we're doing that show – the importance of celebrating minorities in particular Black artists in this instance on the radio – correlation with dance music's roots, I really used it as a way of expressing something good in a dark time. Did a few other bits on *Introducing* – wrote playlists, wrote an article, presented artists, did all sorts of bits and was getting properly stuck in. And that was a pivotal point for me personally and professionally as I'd realised how important it is for me to talk about these things and how much I want to use my platform to support causes I believed in.

Jaguar's unapologetic radio stance and magazine feature firmly puts a spoke in the wheel of the racist media machine. It stopped that ugly turn to let the light shine on those whose legacy has long been overshadowed. Visibility is a wonderful gift.

*

When *DJ Magazine* came out of their four-month pandemic pause, Carl Loben and his editorial team had to do a lot of soul searching. Post-George Floyd's murder, the question wasn't just if they were covering Black music enough;

the identity and structure of the magazine was in question. Was their editorial team and general staffing equal and diverse? Carl had always tried to be anti-racist and anti-sexist but found that the whole process of addressing their unconscious biases and delving more into history was really important. They returned with the special issue magazine in August. All this stuff had happened and they couldn't just ignore it. In the wake of George Floyd and #blacklivesmatter, it felt like the right time to tackle the biases and stats head on. There was a phenomenally positive reaction to my feature with Anz when it went into print and the reprise six months later was a welcome refresher.

The issue contains a pledge to the readers to 'fight harder to reflect the Blackness of dance music'.

Carl explains:

> It's important to recognise everybody's contribution to music history.
>
> We became increasingly aware that the majority of our writers are white male staff. So we initiated a company pledge to move towards a place of equality. We appointed Mick Wilson as our Diversity and Inclusion Officer. Now every three months he compiles a report that we publish on our website, so that our readers can assess how and whether we are meeting the targets and elements of the pledge.[12]

The pledge also promised outreach and community action projects and the magazine has partnered with *A/Z* mag and writers of colour to hold workshops and widen their writer base. And if the writer base becomes more diverse, guess what – the readership will follow suit.

Speaking of which, this year, John Burgess and Paul Benney[13] returned to the print world with their twice-yearly magazine *Disco Pogo*. Its mission statement is to bridge the gap between the new generation of dance music and the best electronic artists from the past. The first issue had Sherelle and Gilles Peterson on its double cover. They're talking about a revolution and changing the world one issue at a time.

You might think it's harder to kill a moving target but there's a lot to be said for being rooted. When your roots are strong the invisibility jig is up. People start to see you, smile and say hello to you in the street. You can relax. Kath McDermott in Manchester and Dulcie in Brighton can both attest to the benefits of staying put. It helps build up your history, you create a wealth of contacts with whom relationships are strong and unbroken (disco divorces aside). You can be an active part of the community. Moving around from Manchester to London to France to Ibiza, created four bridges that I should have maintained equally: you can see what happens when they became neglected. You must stay in touch and keep the weeds out of the garden. I underestimated how difficult relocating and keeping those all-important connections open can be. Twenty years later it's easier. An occasional Zoom, Google Teams, FaceTime, phone call, WhatsApp or an email can make all the difference between working every week and not working at all. Out of sight very quickly can become out of mind.

As big a fan of travelling and experiencing other cultures as I am, I find it bizarre that the Dick Whittington syndrome still holds. The streets of London might be paved with gold but these days you need diamond barter or NFT futures to rent a hand basin in a Hackney studio flat. I'm not pouring cold water on a hot dream, I'm just asking you to think, plan and budget honestly and carefully. With technology and working practices the way they are now it's not essential to live in London to get work there. It helps to be there more frequently when you find your tribe or community and it also helps if you're under the gaze (and mentorship) of powerful gatekeepers and taste-makers. But if you can't get noticed where you are then it is likely you won't get noticed if you move unless you have done something so groundbreaking that the world is watching.

The most painful death anyone can experience is the hung, drawn and quartered torture of your support network collapsing. To explain. When I moved to France, the first two people to support me were Didier Sinclair (Radio FG Artistic Director and France's equivalent to Pete Tong) and Henri Maurel (the President and Founder of Radio FG) – two incredible friends and forces whom I respected deeply. They were superb mentors. I worked alongside Antoine Baduel (President Directeur General / CEO) in the Radio FG office as their International Consultant and I DJ'ed at nearly all their outdoor events. When Didier died of lung cancer the year after my father in 2008, it was a terrible emotional blow that left a hole in our friends' group and a massive void at Radio FG. His post was filled by someone much younger who slowly set about changing everything that Didier had created.

A year later my club residency collapsed when the Directeur Artistique, Ludo Menard, left Mix Club taking me and his team with him. The club closed and reopened quickly with new staff, a new director and a completely new roster of DJs while I found myself out of a job, out of the clubbing loop and the split was so acrimonious that we were all out of favour in Paris. It took a year to find another residency.

Henri Maurel died three years later and by this time the clubbing and musical landscape had completely changed. Radio FG had become more commercial, and my show was being pushed online to 'Underground FG'. I tried production and singing but it wasn't for me. My club crowd had moved on and The Queen was too chichi for my regular fans. My club residency was being killed by VIP / bottle service and my show was being moved around the schedule like a séance glass. My relationship with my booking agent had soured, I had no cheerleaders at the radio station and was so strongly associated with the club and its young audience that it was impossible to play for any other organisation. I suggested a change but no one would listen. Everything that could go wrong went wrong. From this I learned that when you lose your supporters, you're a dead woman walking. It's hard to get that back.

It's a rite of passage in the music industry to be passed over, let go, replaced or fired. Trust me, it happens to the best of us. I've experienced every flavour and none of it tastes particularly nice. If you're intrinsically linked to the outgoing team, no matter how nice or good you are, that undermines your position. The politics of being a resident for one promoter or brand can sometimes stifle your independence. Exclusivity can lock you in a lead-lined box. The lesson here is that it's important to get to know as many people on the scene as possible rather than place your trust in just one. Never put all your eggs in one basket. Things can change very quickly.

Still, no matter how long you have travelled in the wrong direction, you can always turn around. You are not rooted to the spot, and the last time I looked you were not a tree. Or a fish. If you listen to advice, good and bad, you'll find that it's all valuable information. Trust your gut instinct and pay attention to your inner voice; in the silence they will tell you everything you need to know. If it's going wrong, it's best to face it quickly. Adjust your co-ordinates, recalibrate your plans and do something different. Stop trying to fit in like a fat cat in a tiny slipper. If you, your style or your face doesn't fit that's ok, go somewhere where you fit better. You can't always be everybody's cup of tea. So if you stand out, stand out; playing small will not serve you. Learn that everything has its time, its season and its cycle. Everyone has their moment and if you plan well enough, some moments are built to last.

It's hard to keep your fists up when you're gasping for air but it ain't over till you call it. Anchor yourself. Then keep going.

On this subject Norman Jay MBE says:

> The thing that anchored me was Notting Hill Carnival – four million people in three square miles over three days. I fully understood from the early days that those two or three days were going to be our (Black people's) only platform of exposure. We were out on our own. Every bit of money we made went into the sound. Post-1976 I thought what could I bring to the party? I know ... I could bring another dimension of Black music that isn't being represented at Notting Hill Carnival. Then in 1979 I'd just got back from New York – I'd been listening to WBLS radio – Timmy Regisford. I'd heard these records played non-stop, in a continuous mix, played on two turntables. I was all about putting our soundsystem somewhere where people could come safely and hear music. Grand Tribulations became Good Times.

In the face of opposition, it's important to learn how to feel proud. There are some who mistake pride for arrogance or self-aggrandisement, especially when that pride is coming from Black people. It is not these things. Remind yourself that few white men have a problem with celebrating their wins, so it is right, just and fair that you too should remember and feel pride in yourself and your achievements. When you can feel this, resurrection and success is possible, but you have to have the stomach for the work to come. It's not

Welcome to the club

an easy journey and it won't happen in three days. You must be ready to knock everything down and rebuild it from the ground up. You have to be humble; you have to be patient but more important than that you have to keep your head up. Remember who you are, where you came from, what you've achieved and why you do this – this is your anchor through every storm.

In the words of Dr Martin Luther King, Jr: 'Too many Negroes are ashamed of themselves, ashamed of being Black. A Negro got to rise up and say from the bottom of his soul, "I am somebody. I have a rich, noble and proud heritage. However exploited and however painful my history has been, I'm Black, but I'm Black and beautiful."'

Be proud. Shout about it. And if the haters have something to say about it? Shout louder.

The Brownie Guide motto says: 'Be prepared', and it's something we should all take to heart. Also know that if you only ever put the same thing in, you'll always get the same thing out, which leaves no room for growth, so try to change or do something differently – even if it is just one thing – year on year. The cumulative effect of small incremental changes can be huge. So, as Norman Jay MBE says: 'Create. The more stuff that you create the stronger your legacy becomes then nobody can deny you. Look in the grass for the seeds they leave behind and try and make the best out of that.'

Failure is nothing to be afraid of. It contains valuable lessons, so let it teach not define you. The biggest bear traps are stagnation and complacency: these come when you are doing well, yet both signal a lack of enthusiasm and the loss of inspiration. Tend to them quickly because they can do the most damage. Do your homework. Do your research. Be honest with yourself. And clear some bandwidth.

Gym, therapy, meditation, journalling, dancing – do what you need to make you feel alive or anything that might help you to jump start your creativity.

Following my own advice, and with a little therapy, I regained positive forward motion. By 2018 I'd curated a successful exhibition and my bookings had improved. I was travelling overseas again and moving up the line-ups. By the end of 2019 I was on course for my best year yet. But just when I thought it was safe to go back in the water, along came Covid.

6
Sane as it ever was

In February 2020 a new virus was formally named as SARS-CoV-2. The disease caused by it was named COVID-19. At the same time, news was rippling across the Atlantic about an illness that was taking a grip of Wuhan in China but the rest of the world seemed to think there was nothing to worry about. It was an 'over there' problem.

I'm all glammed up and ready to DJ at the Glitterbox party at Printworks in London. On the way to my room, I had a tentative conversation with Simon Dunmore about the virus affecting our industry. He said that it was business as usual but the government was reviewing the situation on a weekly basis. Anyway, the party was a glittering success. Events 1–Covid 0. The next day, my 'Sunday Service' brunch session at Albert's Schloss told a similar story. Grabbing a moment between sets to chat with one of the directors, Neil McLeod, I asked if he thought any changes were imminent. He said that it was a growing concern, but no-one really knew for sure so until the government said otherwise, we were to carry on. Business as usual. Events 2–Covid 0.

On Tuesday 10 March 2020, the emails landed.

Since the virus involved close contact with people and its spread had to be contained, events and hospitality were to close. In Manchester, Albert's Schloss / Mission Mars was one of the first organisations to alert their staff to the imminent changes. All bookings were cancelled until further notice and daily business was to be reduced. On 11 March, the World Health Organization declared the COVID-19 outbreak a global pandemic due to the rapid spread and severity of cases around the world. Over the next week, the entire events industry was shut down indefinitely with a return date that was to be reviewed every three months. The managers of the bars I worked at made emotional closing posts on their Instagram accounts, and their HR departments sent out informative emails to freelance staff with numbers to contact for benefits. I often wonder if I would have robbed a bank or had casual sex instead that weekend, had I known that Covid had just fired the starting pistol on the longest government- and pandemic-enforced, juridic pause to my life, my profession, my career and the entire industry. The shock felt like running full pelt, soaking wet into an electrified brick wall.

There are moments in life that can totally change you, everyone and everything around you. I've been hit by divorce, death, depression and an embezzling accountant but each time I bounced back, blooded but not beaten. None of that prepared me for the timebomb now known as COVID-19. Over the next two years we would learn a lot about mandatory unemployment, benefits, the department of births, deaths and marriages, plague raves, criminal political behaviour, gaslighting, saintly civilian deeds, neurotic conduct, extreme hygiene, sobriety, self-love and self-preservation. We also discovered that we could be Covid winners despite the daily lottery of loss.

The first week of lockdown was hallucinatory – I was generally happy about being told to stay home and not talk to anyone – hell that's what I did every day anyway. The glorious blue skies, sunshine and heat made life deceptively pleasant so being at home alone and enjoying the garden was a joy. I had been working hard and had enough money saved to withstand a short blast; the break gave me space to think and it was a great opportunity to get my house and paperwork in order.

Once Covid was declared a pandemic, it was clear that the government had no plans to support freelancers, the self-employed or the events industry. My fears of a total lockdown, the erasure of my sole source of income, sitting on the sofa with nothing to do and nowhere to go every day, the radio-station closure, total isolation from family, friends and work became a reality. After two sleepless weeks of crushing worry magnified by doom-scrolling on social media, my neck was on fire. I couldn't sleep, couldn't lie down, couldn't stand up, couldn't move and nor could I turn my head without screaming in pain. I suffered for four days then called 111 and was referred to North Manchester General Hospital for an X-ray. I rode alone, curled up in a foetal position in the back of a taxi. Every bump and turn in the road reverberated through my neck up to my brain, down my spine and out through my toes. After sitting like a hedgehog in A&E for two hours, I was X-rayed, shouted at by the technician for not standing straight enough, then sent home with a box of codeine and a neck brace. My friend Anne-Marie joked about covering my brace of shame in a bright Kente fabric. I would have laughed if I could have moved my head without crying. The wedge compression fracture to my T1 vertebrae wasn't diagnosed until late September, but that's another story.

I found myself getting irrationally angry every Thursday at 7 p.m., when the neighbours two streets away had open-door 'clap for the NHS' sessions with Bonfire Night-level fireworks and a festival-volume PA system. My curtain-twitching had ramped up and my noise complaints had gone into overdrive. It seemed like every time I breathed my next-door neighbour's chihuahua lost its mind. The paranoia. Then the family deaths. I became obsessed with journalling. I talked to my plants and opened and drew the curtains on an infinity loop. I stayed in my pyjamas. My car gathered dust, I barely saw anyone in real life and the street had begun to look like a set from *Mad Max: Beyond Thunderdome*. We'd been in lockdown for two weeks, but it felt like a year.

One quiet day in April, while looking at the cancelled dates on my diary, I had my first anxiety attack. It was extreme and came on as quickly as if liquid terror had oozed, like mercury, into my veins from my feet up. I could not move. I was paralysed by the anti-gravity defying weight of it all. I sat with my back against the wall, frightened that I might stop breathing yet hoping that I would. I remembered a grounding tool from my previous therapy sessions – 5, 4, 3, 2, 1 – naming out loud five things you can see, four things you can hear, three things you can touch, two things you can smell, one thing you can taste – and – we're back in the room. I followed the instructions exactly but I remained, muscles frozen, slumped on the floor with my back flat against the wall, jaws clenched, terrified. I wasn't back in the room. I wasn't anywhere I could even name. My eyes were wide open, but my brain didn't recognise where I was. I repeated the process multiple times before the intensity of the feeling died down enough to move less than two metres to sit on my office chair. It had taken me an hour. Once there, I opened my laptop, filled out a personal assessment for Healthy Minds through the NHS website and prayed for a quick result.

Welcome to the club

The red flags were popping up everywhere but I didn't see my constant over-thinking, insomnia or jumpiness around other people as anything other than normal under the circumstances. The clamour and the noise of my peers, DJs and the entire arts and events industry collectively panicking and shifting their lives online overwhelmed me. I felt submerged by the tsunami of Facebook lives, controllers, high-speed Internet, TikToks and Instagram reels. People were taking affirmative action, celebrities were singing 'Imagine' over on Instagram so why couldn't I? I was only obsessed with watching every news bulletin and government press conference while my connection to social media and my phone became like a *Videodrome*-esque extension of my arm. My family could not understand why I hadn't jumped on and embraced the livestreaming bandwagon. 'It's easy,' they said, and each advised me to 'get online and earn myself some money, everybody's doing it'. I removed myself from the family WhatsApp groups. The fear had got to me.

Still there was hope. Nadine Noor[1] invited me to take part in the BBZ x Pxssy Palace online takeover for Boiler Room. I had worked for them previously at the Lesbiennale event in London and I was honoured to be asked. This was an incredible opportunity to put a stream out there for an organisation that already had a captive audience and was making a political point. It was a chance to get back to doing what I loved – playing music and making people dance – even if it was in their homes – so I accepted. The next day my laptop died a white screen death, while my old 2008 backup MacBook was working but on an archaic operating system that did not communicate with the OBS or Reaper software that Boiler Room had briefed me to use. My prototype Traktor S8 did not take USB sticks, which meant my music library was unusable. My Internet signal was not stable enough to live stream. At a time when every pound spent left an unfilled hole in my finances, I had to invest in myself. I bought a Pioneer Controller, which was delivered the day before the deadline for submitting the assets for the session.

Producing the Boiler Room stream was a logistical nightmare. I didn't have anything I needed at home or the experience to do it without some form of help or coaching. We could only take an hour's walk alone for personal exercise, were allowed to leave the house only for essential work or shopping and guests were forbidden. Popping out every two minutes for batteries, cables and such like was not permitted. One friend offered to help with cables, laptops and coaching but he did not come through. Despite these challenges I am blessed to have good friends and people around me who came to my aid. Sam Oliviera and Rachel Roger (the Directors of Reform Radio) loaned me a soundcard, Gina Breeze talked me through technicals, Lee Crank delivered cables, blackout curtains and disco lights on a stopover through Manchester, and Chris Massey was on hand with software and studio connection advice. I wore my bathrobe over some disco clothes, which looks batshit now every time I watch it. I recorded the video and audio as live, and as out of sync as it is, it was well received when it was broadcast.

My first lockdown radio mixes for Reform Radio, BBC 6 Music and Worldwide FM were hampered by inexperience, inefficient equipment and living on a main road. I made loads of mistakes and wasn't confident making my shows for months but I still made them. As I was always on the edge, doing the simplest things was stressful. I cried a lot and learned how to pull myself together for the outside world.

Welcome to the club

The turning point came when Sacha Lord[2] posted on Twitter asking for suggestions for performers for a series of live streams. I had made online friends with a woman called Stephanie Fox who said I should put myself forward for the streams, but I was in such a dark place mentally that I just couldn't. Stephanie tweeted Sacha telling him to book me because 'She is the Queen'. The cavalry had arrived. Sacha emailed me, inviting me to get involved in the launch event at Unity Radio. Gareth Brooks was booked for the opening weekend and I was booked for the following Friday. I stopped thinking about the things I couldn't do and started doing what I could. This was a moment where we had to come together and support each other.

Stream GM came about following constant phone calls between Andy Burnham[3] and Sacha. At first they didn't think it was going to be that bad. They thought the lockdown would be for a ten-week period – little did they know. Andy asked, 'How can we keep people entertained within their homes in Greater Manchester?' Sacha didn't know, then he came across *United We Stream* in Berlin – they had a theatre, and they were putting parties with small residents on and charging 1 or 2 euros. Sacha says:

> I thought we're going to do this on steroids; if you're going to do it, you have do it properly. We needed a risk-assessed, Covid-secure, lockdown compliant venue: they gave me the keys to The Met in Bury.[4] That's where our base was. Andy stuck his neck out. The artists were nervous about driving to the location, being seen on the road, so we had official letters to cover if the police pulled them over. And that was it.

The first couple of weeks were great, then something happened with the first Haçienda event. I don't know what it was, it was a twelve-hour stream – I admit I'd had a couple of beers when we were sat outside watching it. It went turbo – it was the birth of Stream GM in my mind. Over the ten-week period we entertained more than 20 million people and raised £605,000 in donations. I kept out of the financial side of things, but I did see some of the grant applications and they were heart-breaking. That money went a long way to helping a lot of people. It is something I'm proud of. That whole team was brilliant – and that can never be taken away from us.

It was an incredible achievement. In Peter Hook's eyes, the Haçienda livestreams were a way of finding and helping everyone. The whole idea was to be able to do something to aid charities that needed help and it really worked. He says,

The amount of people we reached was frightening – for the first stream we had 4 million, the second 2.5 million and right at the end 0.5 million. We raised a lot of money for charities in Manchester. The Haçienda originally opened so that all us oddballs could get together dressed how we liked, and the streams were a way of keeping that umbrella open.

When asked why he felt a responsibility to help, Sacha says:

I enjoy the role of helping people. In Manchester we saw people pivot very quickly. Mary Ellen McTague[5] had the vision to ask restaurants for their out-of-date produce, then prepared and delivered over 50,000 meals to people side-lined by poverty. That to me says Manchester. I was linked into other cities seeing what they were doing, and Manchester was head and shoulders above the others. Nowhere galvanised the way we did in the North. In the South they sat back, almost like they expected a living. We're real get-up-and-go people and I am quite proud of that.

Out of the fog and into the light.

When 'Parklife 21' tickets went on sale, 80,000 tickets sold out in seventy-eight minutes. Even with stringent Covid regulations in place it was clear that there was a desire and a real need for people to connect again in real life.

Sacha recalls: 'When the doors opened, I saw kids running in and literally crying. It was a big relief and release for a lot of people.' Parklife's success was not without its limitations that weekend. In accordance with the regulations, they left the roof off the tents for air circulation and were accused of cutting corners, they introduced the heavily contested passport system and negative test confirmation and had hand-sanitiser posts everywhere. And no spike was recorded.

For me, the streams and my radio shows gave me a focus, a distraction from my mental-health troubles and a way to connect and engage with people. I worked with an incredible group of brave, big-hearted creatives who stepped up to keep the world and our industry turning. Refusing to be defeated by the crisis, its two-metre rule, the changing regulations, bubbles of two, three or six (outside or inside), moving goalposts, crippling curfews and shifting schedules, we made refreshing lemonade from an endless supply of government-grown lemons, for all to enjoy.

It wasn't just me who was in the medical wars. Lockdown hit differently for women in many ways. Creative Manager of the Warehouse Project, Sophie Bee, was born into the hospitality and entertainment world. A visionary inspired by her father's motto 'You can make anything happen. Just cos no one has ever done it doesn't mean it can't be done. It just means no one's ever done it before', she has worked her ingenious magic on everything from pubs, radio stations and community spaces to some of the biggest clubs and festivals in the world. She credits her best friend Jojo Crago with encouraging her to apply for the Assistant Production Manager post for a NYE Haçienda event in 2014 at The Albert Hall (Manchester). This introduced her to Team Mission Mars and full-time work at Albert's Schloss where her career soared until she took maternity leave at the start of March 2020.

Baby world had been Sophie's news for months prior to her taking time off. She was oblivious to the virus. She had a beautiful natural water birth and her son, Reni, arrived on Monday under a supermoon. Meanwhile Del, her partner, was gigging in London and was due to travel on to Bristol but called to say he was coming home due to armed police at Euston turning everybody back. Two weeks later her maternity leave disappeared into the hole of total lockdown. Classed as 'vulnerable' it was twelve weeks before she saw anybody. Lockdown was, financially and mentally, an incredibly tough time for her. Both being self-employed, the couple had gone from earning two salaries to surviving on maternity money. Her mental health took a hit.

Relief came when she received a phone call in week twelve suggesting her leaving Schloss to work on the project at Mayfield Depot, which was to be called 'Escape to Freight Island'. It was a new concept of safe entertainment that was to open at some point in the future when we could socialise together again.

Sophie says: 'Freight Island got me through the pandemic. It is an incredible concept that helped people to get their footing back in the world.' It was a massive undertaking that, due to Covid regulations, we had to flip the culture of music, dancing, and entertainment on its head to operate. 'Freight Island' put thousands of people back to work and encouraged thousands more to brave the great outdoors and enjoy safe, socially distanced gatherings with music. There were to be no shared condiments. No blankets or heating. Ninety-minute table service turnaround, menu app orders, no dancing or singing and no mixing between groups or tables.

Although she was personally going through hard times, Sophie was bringing joy to people, enticing them out of their Covid-free caves with the promise of subdued but colourful fun and paid employment.

Sophie shudders:

> We forget how frightening that was. I fell through every shit gap. It was an odd difficult time. Everyone was off work when I was, but I couldn't see anyone. Then I wasn't entitled to furlough and I didn't qualify for SEISS [Self-Employment Income Support Scheme] so I realised I had to go back to work and then everyone else was off. It was intense. I was a new mother, with a new family and a new job working with ten amazing but very powerful men as the ideas person for an entertainment complex under strict lockdown restrictions. I was working onsite one day a week and it was very stop and start. All would go swimmingly, then a DJ would play a record like MJ Cole 'Sincere' and the directors would call me to 'reprimand' the DJs and remind them that we couldn't play music that incited dancing. I showed resilience, it taught me strength and it upped my production and bargaining skills.

When I was invited to curate my residency (which I called Paulette Presents 'People Like Us') I was frazzled. After several family deaths, the erratic track-and-trace over-pinging and recovering from my breakdown I had become neurotic about social distancing. Sophie and Damian both treated me with the utmost care, respecting my need for distance, calling me in the daytime to check how I was. She reflects: 'When I have felt at my lowest it's the people who stand with you that you really treasure.' 'People Like Us' was my first foray out of lockdown; it was fun and it ran every Friday for twelve weeks. DJs from Manchester, Stoke, Liverpool and eventually London tried to catch some sort of vibe from the 'no dancing' dancefloor. I knew they wouldn't make a second visit.

I produced two further residencies outside of Freight Island. One for Bruntwood and Home MCR on the Homeground site which was called 'Paulette Presents Together'. Rather than use this as a weekly residency for me, I employed fifty DJs over ten weeks so they could all benefit from some social media love and a little cash. I curated and presented four onstage interviews for Rivca Burns for the Festival Square stage during the Manchester International Festival. Due to government indecision, it was a 'will it, won't it' situation for months, then was green lit at the last minute. All were socially distanced, Covid-regulated outdoor fun in the rain and sun and were all about getting DJs back to work and people out socialising. It felt just like the good old days.

Now I do love a good brunch (and the pandemic was certainly good for such age-appropriate raving) but I am definitely over night-time seated parties. Music is for dancing to. Not dancing to it is frustrating and rubbish, like tying your dog to a tree and gluing your legs together before taking a walk in a beautiful park. There's nothing more joyous than losing yourself to dance in a room or field full of dancers. That ritual release is magic. The pandemic spoiled it for everyone for a while but it doesn't need to do it anymore. The Blessed Madonna and Fred Again made a song about it.[6] I implore you all, please don't lose dancing. Somatic movement is great therapy. I'm not alone in thinking this either. My muse, Sophie, resigned from Freight Island while working for Parklife on 21 September telling its directors, 'I just can't make music for people to sit down to anymore.' Yes, Sophie, you goddess. I can safely say that that post-lockdown sentiment is seconded by me and probably every DJ in the world.

Next to workaholism, it's a common DJ trait to put off anything medical that needs to be attended to until we keel over or someone carries us out. During lockdown this was a real journey as we couldn't get GP appointments and A&E was, well, like an all-dayer without the sounds.

Welcome to the club

After Dulcie's operation and hospitalisation, she found lockdown to be a gift of soul searching, self-love and self-examination. In terms of DJ'ing, events and livelihood, all her work had been cancelled. It wasn't possible to pull anything else together and it took weeks to get her head around the financial situation. She says:

> Normally when we have had a crisis or a recession, we've always been able to consider another territory or city and keep it rolling that way, but because this was global it shut down everything everywhere and this meant that we had no options. Everybody was in the same boat. We had a situation from the government asking us to retrain but there's the hope that we're going to come out of that. By May 2020 that was my darkest point: 'Why am I here? What is the point?' I had to be really brave and ring a friend. It was just so bleak. You're completely out of control. I hadn't had any physical contact with anyone for so long. I cried in her arms for hours and the next day I felt like I had been reborn. I never got any professional help, all that I needed was to cry and sort it out and that was enough for me. Let's take each moment as it comes. And that's one thing I have learned which is great.

The city itself was suffering too. Dulcie and Paul Kemp had had to cancel all plans for Brighton Pride 2020. In financial economic terms, for Gay Pride not to happen in Brighton meant the pandemic had taken a fundamental lifeline away from the community. Pride itself brings in about £18 million in revenue from tourism. When you consider all the people that work for Pride, the contractors, the stewards, the talent and on top of that the fundraising, you appreciate how bad the situation was. Pride was just coming up to the year they were hoping to reach the million pounds on their fundraising. With government cuts in the last few years a lot of those frontline services and charities hadn't received any money apart from the

Rainbow Fund. The city also lost the goodwill and good feeling that the event brings. The whole city gets behind it and gets involved. People come from all over the world, it's one of the key Pride events in the world and the key Pride event in the UK. It makes money for so many of the local LGBT businesses who rely on Pride each year to make enough money to get them through the winter. The pandemic was hard on everybody's mental health.

There's the street party, a park event, volunteers – the parade itself – you're probably talking about five hundred people. It's not possible to move things from week to week. Pride is a year in the planning and if it moves you have to ensure that it doesn't clash with other events happening at those different times. So you can imagine the celebration when Brighton Pride came back for 2022. Take that, Covid.

Preferring to operate in the background alongside James Masters, Paul 'Fletch' Fletcher has been working for the Haçienda for fifteen years (which now gives him the shiniest accolade of being the longest-serving member of staff). He has been promoting nights in Manchester since he was eighteen and is now responsible for the Haçienda tour and brand, Moovin Festival and Barn Party and one-off events. He's someone who always needs to keep busy.

Like most, Fletch didn't realise how serious the pandemic was going to be. He was interested in the story but he didn't really watch the news and didn't think it would be as bad as it was. He only had a few smaller Haçienda shows to cancel and he kept his hopes alive for his bigger Moovin Festival until weeks before it was supposed to happen. When the lockdown was extended beyond May 2020 he had to cancel the festival. One hundred and fifty staff were now out of work and dependent on him for advice, support and direction. Having never had this happen before, he dealt with the daily administration the best he could and started renegotiating contracts to reschedule the acts and move them across to 2021. Would he have to pay full fees? Or would he have to pay cancellation fees for the entire staff? Devastated he began renegotiating contracts and rescheduled the festival for June 2021. It was going to happen.

Fletch says:

> Events take a year to plan. I start to book the next year's festival before the one that is running has finished. I moved it to June 2021 thinking it was ages away then that didn't happen, so I literally moved and planned it three times. The government have no clue whatsoever of what it takes to put an event on. Even bars can't get an opening together in one week. Thankfully the sound, light and tech guys waived their cancellation fees, but even then, the festival we eventually put on was three years' and three festivals' work. We considered doing a socially distanced event but realised that it wouldn't work at Moovin.
>
> We were financially in for a lot of money. I couldn't claim anything and was one of the three million left out in the cold by the government and that does affect your judgement. We were close to losing our house, friends of ours had mental-health problems. It was bonkers. Just the uncertainty and not knowing whether or when it was going to happen.

Feeling a responsibility for his staff, Fletch made a point to phone someone every day. He was conscious that some of his people were lost and didn't know what to do.

When Sacha suggested streaming he was ready. Fletch loves the inception of an idea, decided to make it an all-day party from midday till midnight and really go for it. A few phone calls later, Fletch had secured an incredible international line-up for the Haçienda May Bank Holiday stream.

> The hype was building. And when we went live we broke the Internet. Everyone logged in at the same time. It was at this point where we realised lockdown was more serious.

> Our stream had become something people really needed: that bit of unity.
> I actually cried at one point when I saw the interaction around the world. The love and response we got off that stream was amazing. We raised a lot of money for charity.
> The work Colin McKevitt and the United We Stream / Stream GM team put into our stream was insane. Sacha orchestrated it and pulled a lot of favours. There was that spirit of everyone pulling together. We all love it; it's family and we created something really special.

In the name of resilience, altruism and resourcefulness, once again Manchester came out on top. The livestreams were so successful that they helped to keep the Haçienda brand fresh and in the public consciousness. It's hard to do things outside of Manchester and pushing a Manchester brand in London is super-difficult. Fletch tried for years to find London locations for a Haçienda event. He says:

> Without the streams I don't think the Warehouse Project, Beams or Tobacco Docks events would have been as big as they were. To get that, to do it in the right way, is a massive result.
> The Victoria Warehouse event was a socially distanced experiment. We were still under Covid regulations, so where normally the capacity would have been heaving with 2,500 people instead we had 500 people sitting behind barriers at tables in groups of four. No one could dance. It was an event that was tailored specifically for fans, crew and performers. It was not a money earner – it was more about employing people and getting back to some kind of normality and it did just that.

When lockdown ended there was a real appetite for events. But even though July and August were steady, new festivals popped up with similar line-ups and new promoters which had a knock-on effect on ticket sales. *Resident Advisor* reported that there were 66 per cent more live outdoor events than pre-lockdown. Despite the challenges and the stress, Fletch loves it. He says, 'I'm totally talentless and can't play an instrument but I can still make people dance.'

July brought my full mental breakdown. While I was happily bouncing about, dancing, smiling, writing signs and showing no sign of illness on the streams, at home my mind was in meltdown. I was binge watching, not sleeping, comfort eating, not leaving the house for days at a time.

I wasn't the only one who was struggling. Worldwide FM *Breakfast Show* presenter Erica McKoy described her lockdown journey as 'a heavy time'. She recalls:

> The outside world was really feeling it, there were a lot of deaths, DJs dying. Doing the morning show at that particular time I felt I always had to talk about it. I'm a positive happy person, but it was starting to weigh really heavy. That's what spun me. The motion was already there – someone asked me to do the radio show and I was like 'Who am I?' And then the pandemic spun me career wise and that's when I came off WWFM for a year. Mental health for me is the primary – you can't really function if you're not really healthy.

This is the truth.

We were teased with normality and then it was swiftly taken away. Battling through the pain and the collective trauma of this carrot-and-stick temptation was exhausting. Music was my shield, therapy was my sword. I'll never understand why there is still so much stigma around therapy. I couldn't have come through lockdown without it. I was ill and it helped me to get better. Music is the love of my life, without my relationship to music my world would be unimaginable. Unbearable. It's the medium that has enabled me to express myself and find my community for my entire life. The threat of losing that was something I would not entertain or tolerate.

The most powerful weapon against stress is the healthy mind's ability to choose one thought over another. Yes, I wasn't working but it wasn't my fault. None of this was my fault. Yes – I am a DJ. And yes, I will play music in public again and make people dance. I fought my negative self-talk daily to break down the barricades that the Covid challenges and regulations had thrown up around my work. I decided to distract myself by learning. I'd never had to think about how the sound was recorded, how the studio was set up and why, what times were better to record, sound proofing. I failed massively for the first six months. My first show for Worldwide was so rough my friends called me up to turn the mics down. I struggled with the practicalities of making radio shows from home when you live on a main road. When I think of how I started and how it's going it's a different world. Before I constructed a vocal booth out of duvets and cushions and waited till daybreak to do a voice drop. Now I plug in and speak whenever I need to. LOL.

Was it the music or the lack of music that was making me ill? It soothes me to read that it's not music that makes you sick; 'it's much rather the process of working, music as work, as labour and the conditions of musical work that are impregnated, entangled and embedded with all the misogyny, racism and hyper-competition that we find. It's really exaggerated in creative industries but music is an exemplar. There is an entanglement of music making and mental health just as there is an entanglement of music and wellbeing.'[7]

Coming out of lockdown saw a release of feelings and vulnerability that I had never witnessed before. People were sharing their deeply personal experiences and it was beautiful. Communication and talking like this helped me on my road to recovery.

My first recommendation for wellness is controversial. It's sobriety and the rejection of toxicity. I used to consider myself a happy drunk. It went with the DJ territory. Then things started to happen that made me reconsider whether it was good for me. A friend died of cirrhosis-related complications at a young age. I saw pictures of my old apartment in London with its row of champagne bottles on the floor. I found my Nicolas loyalty card when the shipment of my belongings arrived from Ibiza. I remembered that my weekly order was 3 bottles of Pouilly-Fume or a Viognier (white), three bottles of Bordeaux or a Pic St Loup – l'Hortus being my number one favourite red wine from Montpellier / Languedoc and two bottles of Ruinart champagne. I enjoyed drinking – and then I realised I enjoyed it a little bit too much. A birthday binbag full of wines, champagne and spirits marked the start of my journey to sobriety. I've had one relapse and the associated savage hangover after Parklife 2018 sealed the deal. I haven't drunk another drop. No more hangovers for me. Sober since 2018. This really helped me, and I am proud of myself for maintaining it.

I have developed some bad habits during lockdown that have now passed their use by date. I worry the most about my phone addiction. It begun with Covid, ramped up with the daily press conferences, and now Twitter and Instagram are like crack to me. I also wish that I wasn't so obsessed with imitating Reels audio: I know that's just weird but I can't stop. I try not to check my phone before breakfast or bedtime; if I do I can guarantee the doom scroll is strong. Taking the phone into the bedroom is a recipe for instant insomnia – leave it in another room. As soon as I'm triggered into feeling alone or less than by absorbing people's perfect lives on social media I switch my phone off. I've learned that no good comes from comparing yourself to anyone else but you. Relaxation techniques and sleep? Yes, more please. I love walking, love parks, but I don't go there enough. Once I've finished writing this book, I promise I will walk in the park, use the gym more and get out in nature. Sigh. Does an Apple Watch make you do more steps? Asking for me. I think I'll save this list for New Year just to give me time to psych myself into it.

Some people got it right through lockdown. For Jaguar, Covid and the pandemic helped her to chill out. She got back into reading, joined a book club, read before bed. She gamed: nostalgic games that she used to play with her brother – she was not looking at her phone and tried to exercise a couple of times a week. She spent quality time hanging out with her partner Lucy. Spot the difference. You can learn something good off everyone you meet.

The end of 2022 approaches. I have had Covid once and am quadruple jabbed. I do yoga with Adriene (YouTube) when I can. People have gone back to their offices; my Twitter stream is quiet now that people have gone back to work. My next-door neighbour's dog still barks but I don't want to barbecue it. I also don't feel like I want to bulldoze the happy clappers' house: so life is definitely getting back to some kind of 'new normal'. Scientists report that new variants of Covid will continue to develop over the next six years but I am confident that we, as a people and an industry, have learned to anticipate the changes, to move quickly, to be flexible, adaptable, resourceful, resilient and creative, and that we are now more capable of crushing that and any challenge.

Walter Bagehot writes that 'The greatest pleasure in life is doing what people say you cannot do.' After my experiences during lockdown I know that the greatest pleasure in life is doing what I think I can't do then helping others to discover the same. I can also reveal that if anyone needs any hand sanitiser Sacha Lord and Fletch have got loads in their shed.

Should you ever be faced with another pandemic, I advise that you refuse to be beaten by it. Set your mind to victory and the dark days will pass. See it as an opportunity to do things you never had time to do. Learn a new software, a new skill, bake some sourdough if that's your thing. Network and make new friends – you have a captive audience. If life knocks you down find a stick to help you to get back up and then whack it like a piñata if it tries to do it again. There's never a good time for illness, loss, grief or failure so be gentle with yourself when it comes. There will be much talk of 'pivoting', 'strategy change', of postponements, poverty, cancellations, hopes raised and dashed, mental-health crises, nervous breakdowns and breakthroughs. Don't panic. Prepare for the worst and celebrate the wins no matter how small. The pandemic was what happened, lockdown was what taught us, and what we did with it (and ourselves as we went through it) made a difference to someone or millions of people and that is a truly beautiful thing.

My handsome dad – young Walter George Finlayson in Jamaica, year unknown

Mum's 80th birthday at Cranage Hall, De Vere Cranage Estate, Cheshire. Back row (L to R): Paula Burdess, Me, Elizabeth Cameron, Audrey Wright. Front row: Elicia Clancy, Jennifer Finlayson, Blanche Finlay, Rhonda Finlayson, Robert Finlayson

Promotional image for ACID HOUSE – Steve Vertigo's In Conversation Salon event

Good Trouble Maker

Promotional image for Four Women: a collaborative project based on Nina Simone's song featuring DJ Paulette, Shirley May (poet), Yemi Bolatiwa (vocals), Maisha Kungu (dancer) and Seren Marimba (contemporary circus performer). The piece explores the experiences of Black women within the creative industries and society at large. The music performed by The Untold Orchestra is composed by artists including AFRODEUTSCHE, Errollyn Wallen, Jessie Montgomery and Daniel Bernard Roumain

Promotional image for exhibition Suffragette City: Portraits of Women in Music, 2018

Me with DJ / Producer and Sprechen label owner Chris Massey at the Koffee Pot before the shooting of our Sheroes video

Leaflet for Homebird, 2018

A portrait that pops

Anne Marie Bigby, me and Gilles Peterson at the inaugural We Out Here Festival, Abbots Ripton, 2019

Sequin sparkle through lockdown: the stream for La Discotheque with Stream GM

'Love Is Not Cancelled', wearing a gold sequinned mask during the livestream for La Discotheque / Stream GM

Representing for Flesh in the livestream for the Haçienda / Stream GM

Black-and-white still taken whilst shooting 'Distant Future', a short film about people and the pandemic produced during lockdown

Line-up artwork for Paulette Presents Together, 2021

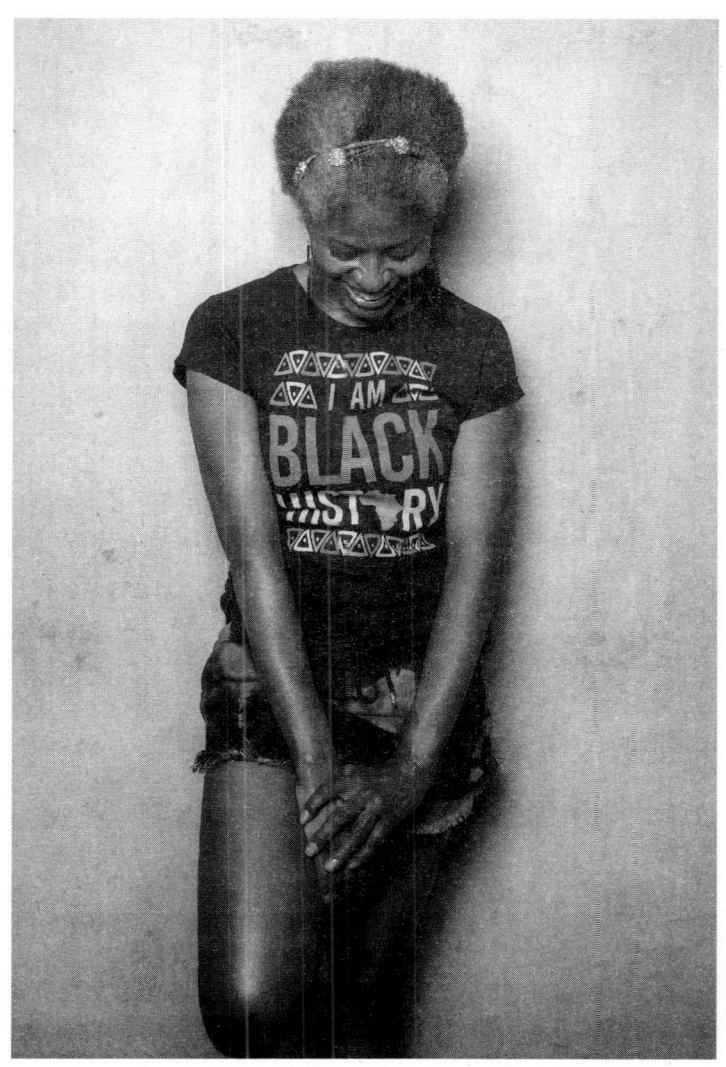

I am Black history: living authentically and unapologetically

Nicola Davies, Jaguar and me in the *Mixmag* / *The Face* offices, recording the Sky News piece for the Progressing Gender Equality in Dance Music Report, London, 2022

Promotional image for my performance during the Musicians' Union Conference, 2022

Poster for the Hacienda event at The Beams in London, 29 October 2022

Flyer for All Back to Minehead

Pops Roberts – a fierce future force, October 2021

The unstoppable Sherelle

7

Lifetime VIP: a manifesto

Among the random children's books that I keep on my shelf, you'll find a copy of Roger Hargreaves's *Little Miss Star*, nestling next to a Gay Pride clack fan and the stuffed Sergei meerkat who was my only company (besides my plant collection) in the beginning of the 2020 total lockdown. I can't remember now whether it was a 2004 London leaving or a 2006 40th Birthday and Christmas present but I do know it was part of a set gifted to me by my dear, departed friend Colin Hinds (RIP Lentil). He altered the title page with a little dedication so that it reads like this:

Paulette is ...

Little Miss Star
By
Roger Hargreaves

You know it.
X Colin

Little Miss Star is a thrilling page-turner. I've read it so many times that it's dog-eared and it always delivers. Little Miss Star, the main protagonist, is driven by ambition and desire, powered by courage, daring and creativity to break out of her humdrum life and realise her dreams. While I've never rabidly wanted to be as famous as she does, her instincts and self-belief are on a par with my own. I've always believed that I would write a book about my life, so did Colin, and as Roger Hargreaves says: 'And here! You are! Reading it!'

It won't have fast-tracked my entry to VIP rooms, first class lounges or any club, for that matter, and it probably hasn't raised my position in the DJ rankings either, but that was never my aim. It does reveal how and why, after thirty years in the business, my career has endured through the peaks, troughs and trends; why my history is celebrated, and that I continue to use my experience and knowledge as an active and passionate contributor to the electronic music community.

Over the last thirty years I have evolved and grown. I've won awards, earned seats at various tables and have secured name checks in the books, music bibles and the revisions of bibles that matter. My love and passion for music and DJ'ing remains obsessive, undaunted, inquisitive and enthusiastic. My DJ diary is full of important headline gigs. I am broadcasting, mentoring and teaching, motivating others to do the same. Reaching our full potential is the journey and finding our purpose is the goal – there is no time limit. Life goes on and my herstory continues.

Audre Lorde says: 'It is in looking to the nightmare that the dream is found.' In writing *Welcome to the club* I confront the central theme of 'visibility' from 'Undoing Death's Work',[1] which resounds today still, suggesting that this rebellious culture, which was once so adamantly anti-establishment, now mirrors society and the corporate, principally patriarchal structures and systemic practices that it originally denounced. My hope is that this book embarrasses (okay, encourages) the DJ boys' club into throwing its doors wide open to admit, acknowledge, appreciate, embrace, make space for more of and recognise the significant contribution made by women, people of colour and other marginalised communities who created this scene and continue to make it so varied and rich, culturally and economically. We have more than earned our membership but we won't beg for space at the table. Men aren't the only humans who can handle a flat pack from Ikea. We can assemble our own.

I encourage admissions from the future-forward generation, which is fearlessly challenging the industry to change and not view their initiatives as existing apart in a separate, sparkling new wing. Working on itself from the inside-out is a foundation that this club and culture should embrace not shy away from.

There is nothing greater than to do something for others. You have what you have *because* of others. In an increasingly selfish and self-important world, acting on this is a radical move. Community is everything. Language has the power to help others navigate an otherwise oppressive world. Your words can be loud enough to wake a house that is sleeping and does not want to be disturbed. Our words and deeds 'undo death's work' by bringing those hidden histories out blinking into the light and putting our faults under the microscope to offer healing where there is hurt. Fact-checking, correcting errors, highlighting those damaging, indelible inaccuracies and omissions will halt the persistent celebration of that false past where the majority of cis males created this culture. There are many female pioneers who also drew the map. If this is the house that Jack built, then Jack had a lot of help and took all the credit. Culture does not create people; people create culture and since we get twenty-three chromosomes from each of our parents, it is both men and women, gay and straight, Black and white who have contributed to electronic dance music's phenomenal epochal change. Frank Broughton talks about the demasculinisation of language: I say can we find other ways of saying 'head honcho', 'godfather of house'. We need to read about and hear about more mothers but there's an obvious issue – what are the female terms, even? The real power is – has always been – and will always be collective and equal. This is the house that *we* built.

I've never been one for pity parties. I make allies of fear and failure. In the darkness I found my higher purpose: a full heart, renewed faith and unwavering passion. And even though it's not my favourite flavour, the occasional splash of bitterness has helped me to appreciate the sweetness. History can't be unlived, but with wisdom, faith and courage, the damaging parts of it need not be lived again.

Carl Jung says: 'Only the wounded physician knows how to heal'; as hardcore and painful as this can be, I've learned more about myself by moving back to Manchester and ripping off the plasters. We must have the courage to keep growing, changing and reinventing. Going back is as valuable as going forwards. The support here has been immediate and overwhelming, and I've found a community of deeply altruistic, like-minded people that inspire me daily. I'm living authentically and unapologetically in my Blackness. I'm enjoying using my voice and loving championing the work and deeds of others who haven't found theirs yet. The talent pool here is rich, diverse and accessible, the teachers and mentors are many, and there are far more opportunities. As a community, we respect and value each other implicitly; we care and we listen. My love for music, radio, people and parties – for the people who make them and the people who rave within – is infinite and gets stronger every day.

Welcome to the club

Welcome to the club is a thank you and an appreciation of the magnificent mavericks, the courageous chancers, the happy hustlers and the resilient ravers and rovers (yes even those who return) who have dedicated their lives to honing their craft, spreading the message of peace, love, unity and respect, touching lives, making stars and evolving this culture for others to enjoy.

It is as much a celebration of their work and achievements as mine.

Representing every voice and every experience is essential if we are to project a more balanced image of club and DJ history into the global consciousness and historical canon. Every experience is relevant. I hope that this message rings clear.

Audre Lorde writes: 'The answer to cold is heat, the answer to hunger is eat but there is no simple monolithic solution to racism, to sexism, to homophobia ...' Lifting the cloak of invisibility caused by systemic racism, gender inequality, anti-gay policies and practices transforms shadowy controversy into illuminated and illuminating, conversations. I recommend that we have those difficult conversations. I order you to read and re-read the *DJ Mag* and *Mixmag* Black issues (2020) to remind you that we've only just begun. It's just two years ago when the press, advertisers and everybody else fessed up to 'unconsciously' cutting Black people, women, LGBTQIA+ and minorities out of their editorial, advertising and recruitment practices. Keep asking for the receipts. Keep up the momentum.

For anyone dreaming of a DJ career or a life in music, I say dream big, follow tutorials, find your tribe, make contacts and get involved. I know how hard it is to become something or someone that you can't see, but if that person doesn't exist then you might just be that someone. Step up:

you could be the one to open the floodgates to others' dreams. Oh – and don't be afraid of being the only one in the room – we can't make a difference if we're not in there. History becomes distorted by the simple absence of our foremothers and fathers. If it is missing, then the connection to everything else is lost. Spill the beans, let all the cats out of the bags.

There's no reason why a woman's place can't equally be in house music as it is in the home. It is essential that we break away from the stereotypical shackles and see women as strong, equal role models in every discipline. My contributors are the personifications of such. Each offers a unique insider's perspective and can reveal the myriad paths that you can follow to achieve your goals. Want to start a record label? Follow Jamz Supernova, Lakuti, Anz, DJ Colleen 'Cosmo' Murphy, NIKS and Black Artist Database. Want your own radio show? Follow Jaguar, Erica McKoy; in fact, most women in this book can give you an insight into that. Want to DJ? Follow us. You know the drill. Lived experiences will always trump abstract theories. The knowledge gained from them enables us to suggest real-life solutions. You have to know there to go there. I hope that their experiences will encourage and inspire you to take their lead or follow in their footsteps.

There has been much talk recently of diversity and inclusion, but we know that solving it needs to go further than token Black and Brown faces on the bottom rung providing the white balance for the power-players and decision-makers at the top. For real change to happen we need a transparent action plan that favours equal opportunity and appointments at all levels, that schedules yearly assessment and is open to revision. Policies need A 'Change By' and 'In Use By' date. We all know what happens to promises and resets; it's two years since everyone promised a world of sweeping change after George Floyd's murder. Now I don't know if it's just my glasses but ... it seems to me that we need to set an actual date for this to happen, then we're so much more likely to get something done that we can shout about.

What else should happen to make the industry more inclusive? If managers and agents look to their line-ups, commissioners and editors look to their staff, and record labels and A&R departments look to their new signings and their mailing lists. As for clubs, events and festivals – it's a massive yes to more diverse and inclusive rosters but please give people decent time slots and equal pay packets too. It's no good saying 'We have women on the line-up' when they are playing for peanuts at midday when people are just arriving or 4 a.m. when people are starting to leave. That has never seemed like a fair deal to me.

As Funk Butcher posted on Facebook: 'Just put women on your line-ups. Don't have to say you have women on there. You don't get any brownie points. Women DJs are not 'data' or a diversity Brucie bonus. Just do it and crack on.' So beautifully and succinctly put. I also suggest revising these with an equal number of women and non-binary to men. Sponsorships, brand contracts and free tech the same – give the women an equal share in the brand hospitality and generosity.

Joseph Campbell writes: 'The cave you fear to enter holds the treasure you seek.' Making history is as much about what we do as what they do. I've looked over the precipice and know that nowhere is change more terrifying than when we have to course correct and change ourselves. What we do in the present constructs our future. Therefore, I challenge you to hold yourself and the people around you to account.

I urge you to scrutinise your values before judging those of others. I ask you to investigate and question the ways in which you have erred and failed. It is important to assess the human and financial costs to us and demand that we put personal measures in place to redress the balance. And it is essential to celebrate the wins and the ways in which we have succeeded. If we can't appreciate who we are or what we bring to the table, why should anyone else?

NIKS of Black Artist Database states:

> Through and post-George Floyd, through and post-lockdown we respect the people who came forward and stood for something. Even though at that time you were still a Black person making noise and it didn't change anything, it just meant that we could. Previously we thought that – stand back, maybe I shouldn't say that – but in lockdown we made a point of saying, involving other people to talk about it, wearing it as a message and becoming activists.
>
> I'm going to inspire other people to do the same thing. Without George Floyd nobody would have listened or heard it. It registered because people had to hear and because people became engaged and inspired. The people that did come through made a good case for it. We weren't looting buildings – we didn't burn anything down physically, but we did burn the structure down, we did burn the books and the way of thinking down. That's the difference between peaceful activisms. Burning and looting don't benefit anyone other than the person that takes something but when you do it structurally, politically, culturally and psychologically it benefits everyone.

To be a fully paid-up member of this club means actively playing a part in the story. It means getting your hands dirty. It means being prepared to fail, to fall on your ass, to be side-lined, passed over, excluded, rendered invisible. It means getting back in the ring when you've been knocked out.

Welcome to the club

It's too easy to sit on the margins complaining about the style or achievements of others. It's too easy to criticise the wins of those who are working hard and making their own breaks. Being negative, bitter, cynical or jealous never achieved anything of worth and reflects more on you than who you're talking about. Before you moan or gossip ask yourself what is it that they have that you want? Instead, plan how you can get it too. You'll find that nothing comes to anyone without putting the work in. More than that, if you ask how you can positively contribute, improve, move this along, a world of opportunity will open. The things we do, the way we act and the words we say or write today become the history of tomorrow. Why wait for others to act when we can make that difference ourselves? Why wait for others to tell or correct your story when you can write it yourself and correct them in it? In the words of the poet Mary Walker:

> Even as your palms sweat, know this –
> your body does not fear the speaking,
>
> It does not fear being heard.
> As you stand trembling,
> as you hover on the lip of voice –
> all your body fears is that you might
> stay silent yet again.[2]

It is the least we can do to tell the whole truth no matter what the word count, programme or documentary length allows. We must be fair and balanced in the telling. There is inequity in homogeneity. There is hurt in omission whether intended or not. The more diverse voices that we include the more accurate and inclusive our history will be. In every conversation I've had researching this book, the pivotal point for change is inclusion. We must give equal oxygen to all voices and give people credit where credit is due.

It's important to gather all the threads you need before sewing the tapestry. NIKS underpins this point, saying that 'archiving and documentation are key to keeping stories live'. Own your story – then prove and save it on your social media platforms. URL links are your friend.

Albert Einstein's definition of insanity is doing the same thing over and over and expecting different results. The tendency among people to take a back seat, that 'silent sanction of things as they are' must stop. When we defer complaining about being overlooked to enjoy a quiet life, we are actively saying: 'It's alright, I accept this situation and I'm not going to challenge anyone.' It's critical for the accuracy of history and the sake of our own self-esteem and confidence to ask for – and to get – the recognition and recompense that we have earned.

And ladies, we can't blame men for everything. This is awkward but we women must address and correct our relationship with ourselves and our sisters. Women have historically not and still do not always support women. In acting this way, we unconsciously (or consciously) hand control over to men, effectively locking ourselves out of the house, the club and the boardroom.

When women diminish or reduce the experiences of women, we are sending the lift we ourselves are riding to the boardroom shooting straight down to the basement. Allyship works both ways. It's more beneficial to understand our differences and see these as a strength than to bring each other down or to cut a promising sister off. We'll get further when we can encourage, support, mentor and collaborate. When more of us play, all of us win. We must propose, then welcome our sisters to the club.

Naomi Pohl[3] states:

> There's a big culture shift here. I think having a woman in a senior position really makes a big difference. But I think even now you know that it has been a difficult road, nobody opened the door for me, and said, 'Brilliant, come in, be General Secretary.' It was a lot of barriers and hurdles ...

It's like Nadia Khan says:

> Because things can change quite rapidly you can think you've moved forward but suddenly you look and you see all your management positions are filled by men again; how did that happen? You have to have a really active watching brief on the makeup of committees and staff.
>
> We are changing the way that we recruit. It's already had a massive impact on who applies for our roles, so I hope you'll see a more diverse staff.

How else can we fix this faulty system? Our best course of action is to question everything, not with the intention to undermine, understand or solve it all, but to have faith that when we do, everything becomes clearer, and anything becomes possible. If we can learn how to listen and learn how to speak without offending, it will be a start. If we can find ways to join the positive initiatives together, we can strengthen our community. The stories matter and the numbers matter in equal measure. The stories and the data are crucial. The more data we collect the more efficient we can become.

Practice makes better practice – identifying our weaknesses and working to correct them, and intentionally pushing yourself out of your comfort zone isn't a one-shot action. Ericsson says, 'You don't get benefits from mechanical repetition, but by adjusting your execution over and over to get closer to your goal.' He was talking about playing an instrument, but I think it applies here, too.

If a door won't open, push it, pull it, walk around it or kick it in. Listen to advice but remember that people can be wrong. Identify the blocks to career mobility – race, sex, age, class, colour, look, sound – call them out if you need to and lean into them if you don't. Prepare for a backlash. Questions make people uncomfortable and not everyone who says they support you will help you. Learn to tell the difference. If we are lucky, age will come to us all. Yet while it is expected that the older generation move on to make space for the younger generation we must hold space for the elders. Community is the foundation. Collaboration is the future. Alliances reinforce the chain. When we come together for a common purpose, we share our skills to make change. Lakuti says:

> Even when we programme / curate nights we need to have young and old. We need to be generous in sharing information ... and I encourage the older generation in the industry to really put aside time to foster these relationships. There is a tendency for the elders to stand in the way of positive change – stay for long enough to make a difference but recognise and respect the moment when it's time to make way for fresh talent to percolate through.

Organisations and internships can benefit as much from the knowledge and perspective of experienced employees aged thirty to sixty+. The *Disco Pogo* and *Seen* magazine ethos of making magazines with elders in mind, Annie Mac's 'Before Midnight' concept of clubbing for the older clientele and DJs / artists being open and embracing their age all help to break the taboo, reduce the ageism stigma and explode the stereotypes. The waters become less stagnant and the current will begin to flow more healthily.

At the beginning of 2022, an *NME* online feature was published featuring Nadine Noor from Pxssy Palace on the cover, while the June 2022 *Disco Pogo* had Sherelle on a shared cover with Gilles Peterson. And notably, since *DJ Mag* published their post-George Floyd 'Will Do Better' charter, it has consistently paid attention to sharing the editorial space and cover equally across gender, race and genres. Along with partners Balraj Samrai and Tunde Adekoya, Kamila Rymajdo launched *Seen*, which is (according to its mission statement) 'a Manchester-based print and online magazine dedicated to counter the London-centric narrative that often dominates music journalism, with an anti-racist aesthetic and diversity-minded manifesto'. Bill Brewster and Frank Broughton's book has been revised. This gives me a deep sense of relief and a renewed confidence that our industry is encouraging inclusive, original, deeper, better-informed thought from a more diverse group of publications, sites, editors and journalists. NIKS and Kay Ferdinand (Black Artist Database) continue with their expansion into more media areas. It's a long-awaited counterbalance to the time when the world and the industry wasn't listening, supporting or nurturing our talent and for the loss of those fallen stars not blessed with resilience.

Black History Month is all about those people in our past, present and future who push it musically, politically and socially by being brilliant, by owning their space and being vocal about all of it. They are the people who stand for something and know how to stand up for themselves and others. I asked my contributors who their fierce future forces are and this is their list (see Appendix). Put some respect on these names. Rest assured, if they're coming through, paving the way along different paths, it makes it easier for everyone to come through, to diversify and to continue.

Nia Archives

Unstoppable. Multi-award winning: MOBO Award, BBC *Introducing*, shortlisted for the BRITs. On every magazine cover. Junglist. Her future is so bright – 2023 will be incredible.

Jaguar

Jaguar Foundation, Gender Report, Future 1,000, BEMA

Radio 1 *Introducing Dance* presenter, *Mixmag Weekend* editor, Jaguar describes herself as 'never the loudest in the room'. She has a quiet maturity, a zesty love of life and a feisty fearlessness about her. Jamz Supernova says: 'Jaguar reminds me that you don't have to wait to be somewhere to give back. I like what she's doing about raising up voices and using her platform for good.' This was the result of a shift in her thinking during 2020 and realising that she can do good in her work. She says:

> I don't want to just play music and jump around. I found my purpose. I wanted to do stuff to help people. 2021 – in collaboration with Virtuoso I launched *Future 1,000* a course that aimed to get 1,000 female, trans and nonbinary students into electronic music. I felt really excited to get something completely different out into the world which showed where I want to go. I'm never going to be the loudest person in the room. Through my work is how I can channel what I believe in and do things for causes that I believe in and I guess more activist stuff. My work is activist-esque but I don't consider myself an activist.

Following on from Future 1,000, Jaguar launched the Jaguar Foundation in conjunction with the Sony Music Social Justice Fund with its mission to make electronic music a more equal space. In 2022, I was invited to take part in a discussion concerning the particular challenge of women, trans and non-binary people in UK electronic music, and what can be done about it. This discussion was one of twenty-six that contributed to the first official report of its kind 'Progressing Gender Representation in UK Dance Music'[4] written collaboratively by Jaguar, Nicola Davies and Daisy Avis-Ward.

BEMA

BEMA (Black Electronic Music Association) is a UK collective dedicated to highlighting electronic music's Black roots. The founding members – Heléna Star, NIKS, Hannah Shogbola and Jaguar – were instrumental in introducing a dance music category to the 2022 MOBO Awards.

Black Artist Database

Created by NIKS and Kay Ferdinand, BAD started as an Excel spreadsheet in May 2020 in response to the pandemic and George Floyd's murder; they saw this as a way of constructively channelling their energies into something positive that could help. On the first day it jumped from 30 artists to 600. May 2021 – it developed into BAD in just over eighteen months based on voluntary work.

NIKS describes the process:

> A lot of the time it boils down to taking a risk and believing the idea you have will be relevant, useful and effective for the people who use it. When you're in it you're so in it you don't have the time to take a step out and say wow look what we've created.
>
> Bandcamp were waiving their fees every Friday – we thought why don't we make a list of some Black artists and

share it among our immediate circle of friends then more money will go directly to the artists.

We made a Google spreadsheet – BLM Bandcamp with obvious names Josey Rebelle, Black Coffee – 30 names on the sheet, then I posted it on my Insta, FB, tweeted it and went to sleep. Next morning, I woke up there were 600 names on the sheet. I messaged my friends – they were like – I went to sleep it wasn't me. On Google spreadsheet if you are not an official editor it names you as an anonymous animal.

There were over 100 anonymous animals in the spreadsheet. There are people who I don't know how they have got hold of the sheet and are as motivated and enthused by it as we are. Shit – on Insta the post had 600+ likes and over 1,000 reposts. We were sat there watching people live typing. I was in awe. I was like what have we done, what have we created. It was so deeply emotional in a positive way. I felt moved. Oh my god it's not just us who feel like this. There's a global feeling of people feeling powerless and thinking what the hell is going on. That happened – then it linked into Bandcamp Friday people still sharing the sheet – *Resident Advisor*, *DJ Mag*, *Mixmag*, *Dazed and Confused*, *i-D* mag, *Vice* – all these big publications had done a big write-up and shared the sheet. DJs – how did they get their hands on this? Carl Cox shared the sheet. Everyone was on the same page, everyone was pissed off and what we did was in our niche underground world provide a platform to contribute towards in a way to support Black artists better.

A Google spreadsheet is not stable – we needed to lock it so created a basic Black Bandcamp website. BlackBandcamp. Info. It meant that people couldn't delete or change it. People would submit their details, we would filter through submissions and then upload them to the site. We had a lot of DJ volunteers who were not touring and wanted to use their time to help. We integrated the backing of Bandcamp into the website so you'd have Kerri Chandler on our website and it would click through to his page on Bandcamp and it started to evolve. It was a really rapid evolution.

In May 2021 we're going into the thousands and it became Black Artist Database. A lot of people were saying – I don't use Bandcamp but I use Beatport or Juno so we reached out to them and we were now in the 4,000 mark.

NIKS and Kay made history. They pushed themselves out of their comfort zone, fearlessly went up against the corporations, interrupted / disrupted the status quo and created a viable tool that they and others can benefit from. They created a structure and a platform for Black people that did not previously exist.

Naomi Pohl

The first female General Secretary to be elected to the Musicians' Union serendipitously on 7 March 2022 (International Women's Day) set up the 'Safe Space' initiative and information resource that is open to members and non-members.

> When the #metoo movement started and during the Weinstein case there were a lot of similarities with the music business and we were starting to be asked if the music industry was going to have its own #metoo movement. People are waiting for a big case. There have been multiple cases that have been quite high profile – but a lot of the cases that have been brought to us, people are making reports because they want to take part in the campaigning work – they want to contribute to what we're doing by saying this happened to me, it's not okay and I don't want it to happen to anyone else; or they are looking for some form of support or advice. We do offer legal advice.
>
> We started it because we wanted to get a sense of how big a problem it was in the music industry and where the issues are occurring – is it gigs, festivals, recording studios, orchestral sector, music education – students? It turns out that it's everywhere. We might have had an idea of that, but we have now got a clear picture that that is the case. It is an ongoing issue; it did not stop during the pandemic, we were still getting a lot of reports and we are doing a lot of campaigning work still.

When I first started talking about this within the music industry I kind of hit a brick wall because people didn't want to hear it – the general feeling was we don't want the music industry to look bad or like it's not safe but guess what? It's not safe. It's been such a massive piece of work ... The Union's 'Safe Space' service for survivors of sexual harassment is my proudest achievement to date.

Anz

From the MOBO Awards and Best of British DJ Nominations, from Ninja Tunes to OTMI (Otras Mitades), from Red Bull 'Normal Not Novelty' to waking the world with her NTS *Breakfast Show*, Anz is an innovative new school, multi-genre artist/producer. She's also a fabulous DJ and an activist. We love Anz. She knows what she needs as an artist, and she is not afraid to voice that. She knows her worth; she knows how good she is and that's why she is where she is. She also doesn't play into the social media game. Mega star.

Sherelle

The Block 9 set with the highest attendance in 2022 was played by Sherelle. Her musical styles range from Jungle, breakbeat, acid house and footwork. She has two record labels – Beautiful and Hoversound and is the Reprezent Radio, Boiler Room and *Mixmag* Lab queen. LGBTQIA+ activist. Eternal raver. A quiet storm travelling at 160 beats per minute.

Nadine Noor

Activist and co-creator of The Pxxssy Palace trans-body positive collective and events and the Overflo festival.

Welcome to the club

While there isn't a rose quartz or amethyst crystal big enough to cancel out or fully discharge the negativity I've experienced over the years, it has always inspired me to press on, to change, to work on myself, to find strength in adversity and reinforce my faith and belief in myself.

During a Twitter conversation on the music industry, Mistajam posted this reply to my comment about following your passion:

> This industry is BRUTAL at points. Without passion for the reason why you got into it in the first place, it will drain you too much. The key is to keep connecting to that passion ... and allow that to help power you through.

You don't learn to deal with shit by having a good time. Rough patches are part of the deal. We overcame the enormous pressures of a pandemic, of huge economic collapse and government abandonment together. Together we have forged a new future out of a disaster which initially threatened to bury our industry. The pandemic magnified our sense of mortality through loss, grief and a slow rehabilitation on every level. We learned that we are more powerful in our humanity when we learn how to do better together. We held each other up, we checked in. And in a strange paradox, the pandemic showed us how to be kinder to ourselves and to each other. It showed us that we could live differently. Peter Hook commented:

> Lockdown funnily enough has shown me the benefits of a quiet life. [As an artist] ... you run around grabbing every opportunity – you're always grasping, clutching anything and lockdown showed you that you didn't have to do it. After chasing your tail for so long – learning the benefits of a quiet life are legion. Looking at yourself and the people around you and realising that they are worth more than you ever thought.

I, my family, friends and colleagues – and this beautiful industry – have become more powerful because we are warriors and survivors. Our survival and growth came through community. If we are to continue to make notable history, we cannot forget those lessons or slide back to the comfort zone of our mindset or business practices pre-2020. We must continue to improve, include and do better.

The fortieth anniversary of the Haçienda, the thirty-first anniversary of Flesh, my thirtieth anniversary of DJ'ing – these are not insignificant numbers. The fall-off of DJs, nightclubs, brands and festivals can be merciless. Some don't make it past one year let alone thirty-one. Longevity, staying up there, the ongoing success of the super brands – Haçienda, Ministry of Sound, Cream, Fabric, Defected, Bugged Out – is a remarkable feat of resilience and planning, the economic benefits of which enrich the economy and support an employment infrastructure that the Chancellor of the Exchequer would do well to examine and understand. And here's a little mantra for you to cut out and keep: when times are bad – plan, budget and save more than you think you can afford, when times are good do the same but more. We all wished we'd listened when we hit lockdown in March 2020. Thank me later.

Be brave. Be the change. Be political. We must not understate the importance of consciousness raising.

Naomi Pohl said, 'You can't stand aside and wait for positive change, you have to make it happen ... Equality, diversity and inclusion is at the heart of my work as MU General Secretary. All musicians deserve equal access and representation from their Union.'

Remember Dom Phillips (ex-editor of *Mixmag* through its most creative and lucrative years and author of *Superstar DJs*) who was murdered in June 2022 for his investigation of illegal fishing and eco-terrorism in Brazil. He knew there was a risk in speaking out about what he believed in, but it did not deter him from speaking truth to power. He died for his principles. Should speaking out deter anybody? No. If we back down on any of this the despots win and a patriarchal, whitewashed, lawless society is all we will have. It is now more important than ever to support the cause and / or have one. Disrupt. Interrupt. Make noise. Be loud.

NIKS (Black Artist Database) is not going quietly. Ever. And all the better for it. She says:

> I'm happy to be the blacklisted person – if that means that in ten years or fifteen years when someone – an eighteen- or nineteen-year-old Black girl is starting, the structure will already be set where it is and better than it was when you started. She is getting booked and properly recognised, forefront of bookers' minds and is paid and booked on equal merit not as a token. The hope is that we are bridging the gap so that in the next decade we would have built something that others can build on and add to.

We can't avoid discussing how we used to live; it's comforting, and it makes us feel fuzzy and warm, but let's not drown in the all-encompassing economic waves of brand nostalgia. History is now, and each of us is playing our own small part in making it and making it happen. I ask that you revisit, revise, argue and debate the contents of this book in five, ten, twenty, thirty years. Use it as a benchmark from which you can appraise where and whether change has been made or if we are still stuck in the same locked groove.

I encourage you to seek out those other stories and places. Research through oral histories. Be aware, when watching, reading and listening, that editorial and directorial bias manipulates stories to keep them in line with the publication or programme's agenda. Doubt everything. Find your own truth. Illuminate then eliminate the shadows that dim the light of others.

One can only gauge its effectiveness when you put it into practice, so I hope our words animate you enough to fire up your engine. Opportunities are valuable commodities that can pass by quickly: hold tight to the good ones as soon as they arise and let the slippery ones go. And remember that no matter how bad it gets, like Covid, it will eventually pass. So, go. Create. If you're able to build some natural momentum and use it positively you will create something beautiful.

The electronic music business is the crazy place where none of us really knew what we were doing but we did it anyway because we loved it, we believed in it and we believed in our capacity to create whatever structure we cared to build. It wasn't a money-motivated decision, although when it became apparent that there was money to be made, careers to be had, and organisations to be organised we mobilised quickly in that direction. That's good business sense. Find that place where your heart overrides your head and where gut instinct creates some of the most memorable nights, successful DJs / artists / music / clubs / brands and momentous events that the music industry will witness. We have ridden the waves of success, turned back the tides of bad fortune and shared our life rafts to the future shore and so must you. There is no time limit. We would do it all again in a heartbeat and none of us has any plans to retire.

A cautionary note.

Claudia Cuseta says: 'Bottle service killed clubbing.'

While Caroline Prothero sums up with:

When the money moves in and the music moves out that's when we have a problem. We have to balance what we're doing ... after EDM came, the years of whitewashing that followed when they cut the Black roots off ... greed is everything that is wrong with that.

Ego and greed are so old fashioned. Community and creativity are in the driving seat for 2023. I ask that you forge as many connections as you can, make them strong and keep them live. An email here, a text there and the occasional phone call works wonders. Always check in with your friends and family. Falling in love with music, people – men, women and those who are both – and parties a little bit more every day is good for you. With patience, understanding and a lot of self-love, you will succeed. Keep believing that through music we can make ourselves and the world a better place.

Thank you for riding shotgun with me through thirty years of my career. When Google didn't exist I'd have jumped on this insider's view into the world I had started to dream about. Had I had this survival kit when I started, I probably would have done a better job, warmed to the technology quicker, been better informed, more politically and socially aware, less afraid, more successful, taken a step back, made less mistakes, saved and invested money and prepared for my future, asked for help, reached out to others quicker and taken control of my career earlier and with a lot less drama. I'd have gorged on the collective wisdom like plump, sweet cherries. Just saying.

Am I welcome and do I still love it?

At the end of the line certain messages ring clear.

I love it. We all love it. I totally buzz off what I do. I am grateful every day that I can do what I love as a full-time job. There is nothing to match that feeling of connection between myself and a crowd that's as passionate, obsessive and excited about music as I am. No matter the challenges, there are no regrets. Passion is the driving force behind it all.

Lifetime VIP

Gilles Peterson says:

> This is my love and joy, it's what I do… If you start at the very bottom you appreciate every element of it. You appreciate the little things that made you think you'd conquered a mountain like tracking down an interview with Chris Hill or being that fan who would go to jazz / funk gigs and wait outside changing rooms to see if I could meet my heroes. The greatest pleasure I get … is actually getting to spend time with the elders and people who give you a human story – meeting people like Steve Reid who saw things a bit differently to the normal way people look.

While our eyes are forward, we must remember that we are standing on the shoulders of our ancestors and revere that knowledge. Listen to the elders, absorbing the wisdom that comes with experience is priceless. Listen to the new blood, the perspective of fresh eyes and ears is indispensable. Each has equal value.

Kath McDermott says:

> What DJs bring is something unique and important. You have to make the decision to do the thing you want to do over need to do. It's a vocation. It's a choice … It's also up to us to pass the baton, to mentor, to teach and to keep this industry turning. What you are creating is your reputation and your reputation is so important. You have to keep your shit together. The way you interact with all of those things will have an impact on you and your career. Be nice and don't be a knob.

When asked what keeps her going, Dulcie says: 'It's just that one person or situation that changes everything.' For Gladys Pizarro:

> We were the seeds that made this grow – I'm so happy that we were part of that. I know it's cool now, but I wouldn't trade that time for nothing. I wouldn't change anything … And I'm ready to reinvent myself. It's not over yet. It's over

when it's over. There's still stuff to do and there's still fun to have. It's just different.

I love house music, I love DJs, I love live music, I love all music, I love women, I love people, I love that through this job I have been able to travel the world and experience new cultures. I love that moment standing in the queue for a nightclub when you anticipate how the evening is going to go, I love the community and families that I have found through it and I love the culture. I love fighting for change, I love the idea that we can all contribute, make a difference and help this culture to evolve until it becomes equal, open, inclusive and diverse. This is the place where I believe, as and when changes are made and barriers are removed, that things will really get better.

About the significance of radio as a future force for good and an essential conduit, Gilles Peterson muses:

> The power of radio and music is still a really important source – as Albert Ayler said, 'Music is the healing force of the universe.' That's our role. The idea of music business / capitalism? I don't know what the future is for that, but for music as a means of therapy it's never been more important and it's a device for helping us to come together. It's unity.

And the thing that keeps our foundation strong? Purpose. Dr Martin Luther King, Jr writes: 'We must discover what we are called to do. And once we discover it we should set out to do it with all of the strength and all of the power that we have in our systems.'

It's essential that we keep telling our stories. History is happening everywhere, to everybody, all the time and everyone holds a piece of the puzzle. In this, we must leave no one behind. Each person I have interviewed has a magnificent tale to tell; dig deep and find out more about them. Be equipped to challenge this story, your story and to do the same with history.

Lifetime VIP

I am Black history. In November 2022 I won the Lifetime Achievement Award in the *DJ Magazine* Top 100 issue. I'm the first female of colour to win among an all-male roll call of previous alumni: Carl Cox, Kerri Chandler, Kevin Saunderson and Danny Tenaglia. Historic. Landmark. NGL – I whooped loud enough to wake the dead when I opened the official email. Every day is Black history. I've started presenting shows as a stand-in on 6 Music and my second *Essential Mix* (for Pete Tong) was broadcast in February 2023. Then there's this book. Long may the work and my ministry continue.

After dedicating thirty years to entertaining people, supporting artists, labels and events, contributing to record labels, press, TV and radio shows, mixing activism with DJ'ing, sending the house-music message to the 24-hour party people from Manchester to London to Paris, around the world and back, I'm looking forward to whatever the next thirty years might bring. 2023 feels like it's about to give me the warmest welcome to the club yet.

Appendix: future forces

Jenna G – activist, singer, radio presenter, promoter

Pops Roberts – Activist, Black Lives Matter to LGBTQi+, singer / songwriter / DJ / producer / educator with independent band project 'Lovescene' which is doing great things. Working on a solo project for 2022

Eves'Drop Collective – founded by Andrea Trout, Li'l Minx and Sarah Sweeney

Li'l Minx – Lover of music, plants and life. Audio Acupuncture show on Reform Radio

Bonzai Bonner – the creative force behind Shoot Your Shot, a highly successful Glasgow-based club event where they occupy the multifaceted role of curator, DJ, performer and host

Queer House Party – DJ collective, community platform and award-winning queer party that's accessible, radical and DIY

He. She. They – Steven Braines and Sophia Kearney

Block 9 – Gideon R3 Soundsystem keeping politics and consciousness in dance music

Little Gay Brother – LGBT festival collective. Founder Clayton Wright.

Appendix

Feelgood Club – Manchester – pushing the boundaries of queer Manchester into the Northern Quarter
LCY
Eris Drew
Octo Octa
Darren Pritchard – Director, activist. Mother of House of Ghetto, Manchester
Rebecca Never Becky – headed by Mix:Stress: Rebecca Never Becky is a DJ and creative collective showcasing talent from Manchester with a spotlight on QTIPOC and LGBT+ artists and performers
Barbie Bertisch – Love Injection Making Music DJ: driven, she's smart
Mafalda
Laura Camer – Amsterdam
Jayda Lorraine
Liv Wu Tang
Mistajam
Funk Butcher – British Council, DJ / producer / songwriter
K G – The Rhythm Goddess – Capital Dance. She's always spotting people and we need more people like that
Taylor J
Aalice
Yung Singh
Shinedoe – DJ and Producer MTM Records. The original Grande Dame of Techno
Brenda Russell – British Grande Dame of Techno
The Illustrious Blacks (NYC)
Quinn from Paranoid London
Jack Said What
DJ Heather – Chicago's finest. From hip hop to house
Rimarkable
Fran Plowright Nelson – Creativity Works / Meet a Mentor

Appendix

Shesaidso – Power Up Mentoring

Colin Peters – Ibiza legend. Manumission, Ibiza Rocks and Pikes residency for over twenty years

Hewan Clarke – soul / funk legend through the eighties and the original Haçienda resident

Mike Shaft – broadcaster, central to soul / funk clubs and all-dayer scene

Eric Powell – Co-owner of Bush Records (along with Eric Gooden) and long-time sidekick of Carl Cox

Discography

Prince – Gett Off (Houstyle)
James Brown – Stone To The Bone
Young Disciples – Move On
Stevie Wonder – Do I Do
Deee-Lite – Groove Is In The Heart
Candi Staton – Young Hearts Run Free
Luther Vandross – Never Too Much
Frankie Knuckles – Workout
Adeva – Musical Freedom
Sounds of Blackness – The Pressure Pt 2 (Frankie Knuckles)
The Source ft Candi Staton – You Got The Love
Terry Callier – I Don't Want To See Myself Without You
Lette Mbulu – What Is Wrong With Grooving
Reprazent – Brown Paper Bag
4Hero – Hold It Down (Bugz in the Attic's co-operative mix)
Koop – Summer Sun
Nuyorican Soul – It's Alright I Feel It
Afro Medusa – Pasilda (Knee Deep remix)
Basement Jaxx – Flylife
Paul Johnson – Get Get Down
KOT ft Julie McKnight – Finally
DJ Rolando – Knights of The Jaguar

Discography

Oscar G and Ralph Falcon – Dark Beat
Yoshimoto – Du What U Du (Trentemoller)
Royksopp – What Else Is There (Trentemoller)
M.A.N.D.Y vs Booka Shade – Body Language
Mason – Exceeder
Steve Angello X Laidback Luke X Rowetta – Be
Lindstrom – I Feel Space
Larry Heard presents Mr White – The Sun Can't Compare
Hercules and Love Affair – Blind (Frankie Knuckles)
Wankelmut – My Head Is a Jungle
Noir & Haze – Around (Solomun)
Bobby Womack – Love Is Gonna Lift You Up (Julio Bashmore)
Kamasi Washington – Truth
Adele – Hometown Glory
Marvin Gaye – What's Going On
Georgie Fame – Peaceful
Aretha Franklin – Save Me
Gladys Knight and The Pips – Friendship Train
The Intruders – I'll Always Love My Mama
Lizzo – Juice
Little Simz – Woman ft Cleo Sol
Beyoncé – Cozy
Janelle Monae – Turntables
Massey and Paulette – Sheroes
Unit 2 – Sunshine (KiNK remix)
Anz – Clearly Rushing
Bruise – The Dassy Slide
Floorplan – We Give Thee Honour
Biscits – House All The Time
Dale Move – Praise
Sylvester – You Make Me Feel (Mighty Real) (Soulwax for Despacio)
Diana Ross – The Boss (Dimitri from Paris)

Acknowledgements

To Colin Hinds – Lentil – you were right. Thank you for seeing the future and making me dream as big as Little Miss Star. Rest in eternal power.

To my mum Blanche, my dad Walter (RIP) and my entire family (too many to mention singularly but you can be sure that I mean ALL OF YOU) thank you – it's your love, care, support and strength that lifts and carries me through. To my friends and to everyone who has contributed to or has helped to facilitate something and to each person who has already been mentioned by name, show, station, magazine or organisation in this book, thank you for your belief, your magic, your support and your generosity of spirit and time. There's an African proverb that says that it takes a village to raise a child: I am so glad and grateful to have been raised by you all in our village. I couldn't have written *Welcome to the club* without you.

To David Watkins – you are a dude! It's been an honour and a pleasure to be edited by one as grand and as decent as you. Thank you for your vision, for listening to my Capricornian speechifying, for the encouragement. Keep the tunes coming, I'll see you on a dancefloor soon.

Acknowledgements

To Emma Brennan, Kim Walker, Alun Richards, Laura Swift, Rebecca Parkinson, David Appleyard and all at Manchester University Press, thank you for everything. I have no words.

To Tom Dark – thank you for springing the lock, teaching me how to corral my stories and triage my ideas. I am grateful for your guidance through the submission and for helping me to secure this commission.

Dear Sam Oliviera and Rachel Roger – I couldn't wish for two more awesome guardian angels than you. My gratitude is immense.

Annie Mac – my heart is full. Thank you for your kindness, humility and your beautiful words.

Kamila Rymajdo – 'have you started writing it yet'? Thank you for the prompts, check-ins, the eyes and our Heaton Park walks.

To the people who aren't mentioned in the book:

BBC 6 Music, AFRODEUTSCHE, Craig Charles, Amy Lamé for supporting me in and after hours and trusting me with your shows. To Rebecca Gaskell, Aisha, Robin Hergé and Ciara at Reform Radio, to Sam Davies and Josh Scarlett at Audio Always, Chris Hawkins, Mary Anne Hobbs, Lucy Darbyshire, Lucy Madge, Simon Ritchie, Carl Hiett and Tarsza – thank you all for the encouragement, podcast and advice.

To Simon Goffe, Noah Ball, Will Asare, Sam Fawcett and Ceylan Goksel – thank you for the Worldwide FM, We Out Here and Worldwide festival love.

To Ali Tillett, Rachel Fairhead and Rachel Craddock at Warm Agency – thank you team of dreams!

To Tim Levy at Limbs – love, respect and thanks always.

Thank you to all at Mission Mars, the Albert Hall, Albert's Schloss, the Sunday Service family – Lucie Rice, Chris Extance, Tim Murray, Dominic Laws, Audrey

Acknowledgements

Lawrence-Mattis. Thank you to James Masters, Yvonne Shelton and all at the Haçienda, Glitterbox, La Discotheque, Joe Spencer, Kat Warburton and Leah Olivia, to all at Defected, Rebecca Rosenberg, Meds Peterson, Helen Kenny, all at Moovin Festival, Kevin Jamieson, Amanda Fawcett, Sekeenat Karim and the team at HOME (Manchester), The National Theatre (London), Peter Dalton, Karen Gabay, Rich McGinnis, Natalie, Damian and all at the Warehouse Project, Anton Stevens, Hidden, Rivca Burns and all at MIF, Kiera and Aimee Lawlor-Skillen, Beau Azra-Scott, *DJ Magazine*, *Faith Magazine*, Boiler Room, He.She.They, Gemma Krysko, Laura Graham, Kobi Prempeh, Khaleel Johnson, Brian McEwan, Paris Armani, Dominique Bellas, Soho House, Keychange and Sound City for the honour, the stage, the crowds, the press and the lockdown streams.

Luke Cowdrey, Justin Crawford, Amy Wainwright, Owain Richards, Jamie Bull, Gina Breeze and Will Tramp thank you for giving me The Refuge and a Homoelectric to call my own.

To Mr Scruff for the 'know your worth' pep talks and invaluable advice.

To Isadora Darke, Paul Quine, Achim Brandenburg and Bury Healthy Minds for keeping my mind and body clear and functioning even when it rebelled against me.

To Andy Jane, Nick De Sousa, Toby Whitehouse and Kriss Herbert at Gaydio, Ant Owen, Sunni Syal, Guy Williams, Gary McLarnan, Martyn Fitzgerald (Handsome) and MiNT Manchester for being the first to facilitate my re-entry into Manchester life.

To the bars and people in the Northern Quarter and Greater Manchester who booked, fed and watered me as I put in a solid 10,000+ hours (and all of those standing) – thank you.

Acknowledgements

To everyone who cleared copyright and authorised photos – thank you for your art, your eye and your generosity.

To Michael Simpson at The Lowry art gallery for setting the wheels in motion with 'Homebird' and for trusting me with your beautiful gallery space.

To the women without whose work the house that Jack built would be missing its load bearing walls: Judy Weinstein, Carolyn Bird, Yvette Livesey, Amy Thompson, Katy Ellis, Maria May, Lynn Cosgrave, Sally Anne Gross, Carol Ainscough (RIP), Dawn Hindle, Jill Thompson, Girls On Top, Heidi Lawden, Olga Zegers, Ornella Cicchetti, Mona Renalis, DJ Debra, Abi Clarke, Sno, Lucy Lockett: I see and salute you, your craft, your graft and your legacies.

To Jon Caine – thank you for making travelling such a laugh and for getting me through train and transport strikes and complex itineraries to play and then get home in time to write and meet my deadlines. You are the best! Now get the snacks in.

To Vince Elgey – thank you for your technical expertise, your laptop loan, your over and above the call of duty back up and your chauffeur level driving skills.

To Emma 'a book is never finished' Warren – thank you for demystifying the writing and the tricky acknowledgements process.

To Walt – the best emotional support dog in the world, you are a lifesaver. True story.

If you checked in or helped me out with reading, listening, advice, care parcels, flowers, cards, Christmas dinner, homecooked meals, collected Amazon packages or anything at all I know that you know who you are and I appreciate how much you've contributed. Know also that I love and

Acknowledgements

thank you and am grateful for everything even if I've not namechecked you here.

And finally to you – thank you for buying and reading this book – it means more to me than you'll ever know.

Thank you.
Peace, love, unity and respect to all.

Illustrations

Section one (pp. 63–71)

Juice pre-series promo photo of Tara Newley, Johnny Dangerously and me, 1993. Photo: Peter Walsh Photography.

Me with my dad standing outside the Free Trade Hall, Manchester on graduation day, 1994. Personal photo.

Contact! Me with Edwin Starr and Roni Size representing at the Brit Awards, 1998. Personal photo.

Me with Azuli Records crew at Hotel Es Vive in Ibiza, 2001. Photo: Ian Usher (personal collection).

Me with Wendy Douglas and Anne Marie Bigby, London leaving party at The Friendship, Kensal Green, December 2004. Courtesy of Gill Kingston.

So happy onstage at One Night with Paulette at Mix Club, Paris, 2007. Personal photo.

A strong look. Lips by MUA Carole Rostaing. Photo: Soyad Mahat, 2010.

Channelling my inner Grace Jones. Photo: Soyad Mahat, 2011.

Illustrations

Up on the roof in La Defense with Vichy, a perfectly Parisian pooch. Dog and apartment courtesy of Sharmeen and Daniel Lalani-Fade. Photo: Soyad Mahat, 2012.

Who's going to know? Paula and me at St Kentigern's, aged eight. Personal photo.

Section two (pp. 163–183)

My handsome dad – young Walter George Finlayson in Jamaica, date unknown. Personal photo.

Mum's 80th birthday at Cranage Hall, De Vere Cranage Estate, Cheshire. Photo: Craig Strong CAS Photography, 2015.

Promotional image for ACID HOUSE – Steve Vertigo's In Conversation Salon event. Courtesy of Royal Exchange, 2016.

Good Trouble Maker. Photo: Lee Baxter, 2017.

Promotional image for Four Women: a collaborative project based on Nina Simone's song. Artwork courtesy of Untold Orchestra. Design by Stanley Chow.

Promotional image for the exhibition Suffragette City: Portraits of Women in Music, 2018. Photo: Elspeth Moore.

Me with DJ / Producer and Sprechen label owner Chris Massey at the Koffee Pot before the shooting of our Sheroes video. Photo: Sebastian Matthes / Manox, 2018.

Leaflet for Homebird, 2018. Designed by Sean Longmore. Courtesy of The Lowry. Photo: Soyad Mahat, 2010.

A portrait that pops. Photo: Lee Baxter, 2019.

Illustrations

Anne Marie Bigby, me and Gilles Peterson at the inaugural We Out Here Festival, Abbots Ripton, 2019. Personal photo.

Sequin sparkle through lockdown: the stream for La Discotheque with Stream GM. Photo by KT Hall, courtesy of Badger & Combes, 2020.

'Love Is Not Cancelled', wearing a gold sequinned mask during the livestream for La Discotheque / Stream GM. Photo by KT Hall, courtesy of Badger & Combes, 2020.

Representing for Flesh in the livestream for the Haçienda / Stream GM. Photo by KT Hall, courtesy of Badger & Combes, 2020.

Black-and-white still taken whilst shooting 'Distant Future', a short film about people and the pandemic. Photo: Charlie J. Watts, 2020.

Line-up artwork for Paulette Presents Together, 2021. Courtesy of HOME.

I am Black history: living authentically and unapologetically. Photo: Lee Baxter, 2022.

Nicola Davies, Jaguar and me in the *Mixmag / The Face* offices, recording the Sky News piece for the Progressing Gender Equality in Dance Music Report, London, 2022. Photo: Jaguar Worldwide Limited.

Promotional image for my performance during the Musicians' Union Conference, 2022. Courtesy of the Musicians' Union.

Poster for the Haçienda event at Beams in London, 29 October 2022. Courtesy of the Haçienda.

Illustrations

Flyer for All Back to Minehead. Design by Guy Pittard. Courtesy of Anglo Management, November 2022.

Pops Roberts – a fierce future force, October 2021. Photo: Jack Kirwin Photography.

The unstoppable Sherelle. Courtesy of One House. Photo: Isaac Lamb, May 2023.

Notes

Introduction: welcome to the club (Belleville or Bust)

1 This, the original Mama Shelter, is an effortlessly cool hotel and hype meeting place with a glorious outdoor terrace and buzzy, vibrant atmosphere prized by creatives, music and media people. Starting at this location in 2008, Mama Shelter is now a chain with locations all over the world including London.
2 Established in 1877, La Bellevilloise is the first Parisian co-operative and the first in France: it is 'une forteresse culturelle' providing access to political and cultural education for all. Since its inception it has played an important role in the cultural and political life of East Parisians. Since 2005, Renaud Barillet, Fabrice Martinez and Philippe Jupin have created a unique independent arts and events space.
3 Frank Broughton – friend, Cambridge graduate, Clubs Editor of *Time Out New York* and co-author of *Last Night a DJ Saved My Life*, who comments later in this book.
4 The Police and Criminal Evidence Act of 1984 extended the 'SUS' laws giving the police permission to apprehend, stop and search any one in breach of section 4 of the Vagrancy Act 1824. This meant they now had the right to arrest people not simply for loitering with intent but also to arrest anyone on suspicion (sus) of committing an arrestable offence. It was not necessary to prove a substantive offence. The Act also gave the police permission to search any vehicle carrying a person about to commit or who has committed an offence. These powers were used disproportionately against Black people.
5 Beyoncé's record breaking *Renaissance* album also put transgender producers, DJs and songwriters into the *Billboard Book of Records*.

Notes

6 References the poem 'Stopping by Woods on a Snowy Evening' by Robert Frost.
7 Before becoming a superstar with *The Big Breakfast, Don't Forget Your Toothbrush* and *TFI Friday*, Chris Evans was an assistant on Timmy Mallet's show on Piccadilly Radio 261 (named after its medium-wave frequency), appearing as the character Nobby No Level. He produced the James H. Reeve show and had a graveyard night-time show of his own before moving to daytime to co-present *Saturday Express* with Becky Want.
8 Chris Whatmough was the Head of Music and John Clayton was the producer of *Saturday Express*.
9 I was resourceful and never needed instruction. I used a similar ploy to confirm an interview with Marks & Spencer and British Airways marketing, securing a picnic hamper with a bottle of Châteauneuf-du-Pape, Champagne, picnic snacks and a return flight to Paris. I made a fantastic feature from that, so I had total faith in my powers of persuasion for a Haçienda freebie.
10 I met Bernie Hot Hot's drummer David Dunne at Piccadilly Radio when he was working as a volunteer on the New Heart New Start appeal and he told me that his band was auditioning for singers.
11 My boyfriend's band KAOS was signed to John Noel's management company. At their record label showcase at SARM recording studios the lead singer got stage fright and I was fired for covering his mute performance with chirpy ad libs.
12 I was among the first to graduate with a university degree when Manchester Polytechnic became Manchester Metropolitan University under the government's Further and Higher Education Act in 1992.
13 Paul Cons (Haçienda Marketing Manager and Director of A Bit Ginger Productions), Peter Hook (owner of the Haçienda), Luke Howard (Queer Nation resident), Kath McDermott Flesh Resident), Ang Matthews (Manager of the Haçienda, 1987–98).
14 Dulcie Danger started at the Zap Club and became a business partner with Paul Kemp, responsible for the Wild Fruit parties. Together with Paul Kemp she is ex-Director and the current DJ Booker for Brighton Pride and also one half of Oxylion and Danger (DJs / Producers) with a Saturday night mixshow on Gaydio.
15 Discovery came through regular trips to Paris for bookings, travelling on the Eurostar, and spectacular appearances at the Ministry of Sound residency at Queen Club, Paris under the direction of Thibault Jardon and Laurent Chaumet.

Notes

16 Benjamin joined *Play School* in 1976, following in the footsteps of Black alumni Carmen Monroe, Johnny Silvo and Derek Griffiths.
17 Quote is taken from an interview promoting her book *Why Are You Here?*, published in the *Guardian*, 12 June 2022. The bowling alley incident refers to a time in her youth when she was beaten up while bouncers looked on.
18 #breakthebias was the theme of International Women's Day 2022.
19 'The Forgotten Women of Rave' written by Heather Saul and Sarah Howell (the *i*, 2018).
20 Kamila Rymajdo PhD – editor of *Seen* magazine, freelance journalist, author and academic.
21 Carl Loben (Editor-in-Chief, *DJ Magazine*), Frank Broughton and Bill Brewster (co-authors of *Last Night A DJ Saved My Life*).
22 Bill Brewster – Former Editor of Mixmag USA, co-creator of the DJ history website and Lowlife parties, DJ, broadcaster.
23 #metoo litigation – Bill Cosby, R. Kelly, Harvey Weinstein, Solo 45, Prince Andrew, Erick Morillo and Tim Westwood.
24 Hashtags – the group-organising framework created by Chris Messina in October 2007. In terms of activism these hashtags are #blm #metoo #lgbtqia+ #timesup #mentalhealthawareness #suffragette100 and #breakthebias.
25 Emma Brennan, Head of Commissioning, and Tom Dark, my first Commissioning Editor at Manchester University Press.
26 Key personnel are Peter Hook, James Masters and Paul Fletcher (the Haçienda), Gilles Peterson (Worldwide FM), Sophie Bee (Escape To Freight Island) and Sacha Lord (the Warehouse Project).
27 *DJ Magazine* Top 100 issue – November 2022 – DJ Paulette wins the 'Lifetime Achievement Award'.

1 Finders keepers: in the beginning

1 The Kimpton Clocktower Hotel – dubbed 'The Ned of The North' in 2019 by *GQ*, it is one of Manchester's more glamorous nightspots, originally curated by Luke Cowdrey and Justin Crawford (aka The Unabombers).
2 CDJ – Compact Disk, Disc Jockey: a digital turntable introduced by Pioneer in 1994 originally made to play the CD format, which with the introduction of the 3000 in 2020 now amusingly runs on USB sticks and does not take or read CDs.
3 An unpretentious gay club situated at 1 Central Street in Manchester that was a well-regarded underground haunt.

Notes

4   A Bit Ginger Productions – the name of the independent production company run by Paul Cons and Lucy Scher which created the Flesh party at the Haçienda from 1991 to 1996.
5   Paul Cons was the Entertainment and Promotions Manager for the Haçienda from 1986 to 1991.
6   Trevor and Craig Johnson designed all the artwork for Flesh and were part of the Factory design team from the eighties, working on Joy Division, New Order and the Haçienda.
7   The Pussy Parlour is the name given to The Gay Traitor for the Flesh party.
8   David Piccioni – Black Market Records / Azuli Records.
9   Thanks to Jean Branch at East West, Johnny Morris at Arista, Vanessa at Deconstruction, Simon Dunmore and Trevor Nelson at Cooltempo, Leo Ryan and Steve Wolfe at A&M, David Piccioni at Azuli Records, Rob Manley and Caroline Prothero at Virgin / 10 Records, Matt Waterhouse at XL and then Matt and Laura at MCA, Johnny Walker at Champion, Andy Thompson and Phil Howells at London / FFRR, Steve Ripley at Sony and S2, Phil Cheeseman and Anna Goodman at Strictly Rhythm, James Horrocks and Thomas Foley at REACT, Nicky Trax at Phuturetrax, Caroline Peady at Island Records, Lisa Loud at Loud and Clear, Marts Andrups at Narcotic (RIP), and Eddie Gordon at Song and Dance for being the first to send records to a new Manchester DJ.
10 *DJ Magazine* is one of the early dedicated industry 'bibles' for dance and electronic music news.
11 'Loose' is known as Liverpool's first queer rave.
12 Namely Trade Resident and Ibiza icon Smokin Jo and Angel from Venus in Nottingham.
13 Manchester Underground was opened by Kenny Grogan, Harry Taylor and Russ Marland in 1992 and specialised in US dance imports. I always had a warm welcome here as Jamie Scahill (then one half of DJ duo The Slammin Boys) would always reserve a bag of the hottest promos for me. It was closed down as a result of an IRA bomb in 1996.
14 Bar Kay was renamed as South and was situated on 4A South King Street. It was later home to Inspiral Carpets keyboard player and vocalist Clint Boon and closed for the last time on 4 June 2022.
15 Michael Barnes-Wynter was known as 'Barney' through the nineties.
16 Leroy Richardson was the longest-serving member of staff and bar manager / manager of the Haçienda and Dry Bar 201.

Notes

17 Situated in Affleck's Palace, Ono Eno was the fashion label owned and run by Eno Eruotor who is now a BBC Broadcaster.
18 The Star & Garter in Bristol holds huge significance to the St Paul's community. The pub has been the inspiration to music legends such as Massive Attack, Roni Size and the late DJ Derek. Since 2019 it has been run by Malcolm Haynes and his family. Malcolm has spent many years as one of the organisers of Glastonbury Festival, founding the Dance Village now known as Silver Hayes. He co-ordinated the 2018 St Paul's Carnival and is a long-time Bristol resident.
19 Tara Newley is the celebrity Joan Collins's daughter.
20 Lily Savage was presenter and broadcaster Paul O'Grady's drag persona.
21 The Zap Club is the legendary Brighton nightclub where the then rising star Carl Cox had his Friday residency.
22 Heaven was then owned by Richard Branson, managed by David Inches, and can still be found under the arches in Charing Cross.

2 London to Paris: Eurostar

1 Whenever a guest was booked, I would close the party and Dulcie Danger would warm up. When we didn't have a guest Dulcie opened, I would play the middle set and we would play back-to-back until closing.
2 Under the creative direction of Wayne Kurz (RIP) I welcomed guests including Paul 'Trouble' Anderson, Justin Berkman, DJ Disciple, Princess Julia, Rachel Auburn, Roger Trinity, Danny Rampling, Tall Paul, Trannies with Attitude, Mrs Wood and Sister Bliss among many others to the decks of my It Girl residency at the Zap Club.
3 Tracks like Size 9, 'I Am Ready', Subliminal Cuts, 'La Voie Soleil', Skee-Lo, 'I Wish', Danny Tenaglia and Carole Sylvan, 'Look Ahead', That Kid Chris, 'Carlito's Way', Hardrive, 'Deep Inside', River Ocean, 'Love and Happiness – Yemaya o Ochun', Bobbi Brown, 'Two Can Play that Game'.
4 *The Word* was Kiss FM's (the London pirate station's) equivalent to Radio 1's drivetime arts, music, celebrity and news segment 'Newsbeat'.
5 I was a regular contributor on Judge Jules's 'Judge and the Jury' record review show on Saturday nights on Kiss FM before I was headhunted for the Press Officer position at Mercury Records.

Notes

6 Janine Neye – Organiser, co-ordinator and promoter of That's How It Is at Bar Rumba and We Out Here and Dingwall's.
7 Bee Sayed – Host and Manager of That's How It Is at Bar Rumba, Production Manager at the magazine *Straight No Chaser*.
8 Rapido TV is one of the UK's most notorious TV programmes, responsible for launching names including Antoine de Caunes, Graham Norton, Johnny Vaughan, and Sara Cox. The famous 'froggie' has trademarked over a hundred well-known series and programmes including *Eurotrash, Passengers, Unzipped, Fortean TV, Naked City, The Girlie Show, Baadasss TV* and *Carnal Knowledge* . . .
9 *Baadasss TV* was promoted as an irreverent but affectionate review of the wilder shores of the globe, mixing comedy, culture and celebrity interviews. It ran for two series and twelve episodes.
10 Eddie Gordon was then the owner of a record promotion company called Song and Dance and the newly appointed Director of the Mercury Records dance music offshoot Manifesto Records. He also managed Pete Tong from 1984 to 2004 and was the creator and Producer of Radio 1's *Essential Selection* from 1991 to 2003.
11 Pete Tong started FFRR records in 1986, and it was absorbed into London Records in 1990. He started the *Essential Selection* on Radio 1, created and produced by Eddie Gordon, in 1991.
12 Andy Thompson was Head of A&R, Promotions at London Records / FFRR throughout the nineties and into the noughties. He was drafted in to work alongside Pete Tong when the FFRR label was revamped and relaunched in 2011.
13 Kas Mercer was responsible for artists including Metallica, Def Leppard, Elton John and Tears for Fears.
14 Dawn Bartlett was the Senior Press Officer who handed over responsibility for press and publicity for the entire Talkin' Loud roster, Dina Carroll, Donna Summer and Oleta Adams to me.
15 Director, Howard Berman, the General Manager, Jonathan Green, Head of Radio Promotion, Bruno Morelli.
16 Director of Talkin' Loud and Director of A&R respectively.
17 The Talkin' Loud upcoming projects included albums from Nicolette, Galliano, United Future Organisation, Shawn Lee, the Nuyorican Soul project from Masters at Work (Louie Vega and Kenny Dope Gonzales), Terry Callier, Femi Kuti and drum and bass album projects from Roni Size and Reprazent and 4Hero.
18 Lamb consisted of singer Lou Rhodes who had taken my photos in Manchester for Sheryl Garratt at *The Face* and *City Life*, and Andy Barlow.

Notes

19 The Manifesto roster included Donna Summer, Josh Wink, Bizarre Inc., Gusto, David Morales, E'voke, Mary Kiani, Definition of Sound, Blahzay Blahzay, Todd Terry, Byron Stingily and many more.
20 A statement printed in all issues of a newspaper, magazine or the like, usually on the editorial page, giving the publication's name, the names of the owner and staff etc.
21 Oleta Adams sung 'Rhythm of Life' 'Get Here' and 'Woman in Chains' with Tears for Fears.
22 Smokin Jo is an iconic, Black female UK DJ and superstar. Resident of Lawrence Malice's Trade party in London, she was one of the early DJs to conquer Ibiza, playing firstly at Space in 1993 then becoming a regular fixture for the legendary Manumission parties which were held at Ku then renamed as Privilege in Ibiza. She had a shaved head, a fierce presence and is the only woman to have gained the #1 slot in the DJ Top 100 Awards.
23 UK Rumbal was a roots / raw 'pirate' online radio station, the studio of which was situated in a dusty Camberwell warehouse. Also noteworthy, the studio neighbours were two young men, Felix Buxton and Simon Ratcliffe, who were soon to become Basement Jaxx.
24 The studio had a black curtain for soundproofing and an ironing board in the vocal booth.
25 Originally a derelict bus garage, the Ministry of Sound was established in 1991 created by James Palumbo and Justin Berkman and remains a trailblazing all-night club and the home of house music.
26 Guests were Larry Heard, Kerri Chandler, MJ Cole, Terry Hunter and Frankie Valentine, among others.
27 Kbps is kilobits per second, 1,000s of bits per second, the amount of data that can flow in any given time.
28 2G is a digital mobile communications standard allowing for voice calls and limited data transmission. This did not include photos, emojis, live chat or Internet use. It only covered phone calls and text messages. 3G handled voice and data more efficiently. 2022 was a 5G breakthrough year.
29 My top of the range Atari ST had an optimum memory of 4MB. In comparison my mini-USB sticks hold 128GB.
30 Word processed documents were printed on single sheets then faxed to the magazine. Microsoft Outlook and AOL started to connect users on a global scale in 1993 but the worldwide take up happened when Hotmail launched in 1996 and Yahoo followed suit in 1997.
31 Largely Black and people of colour.

Notes

32 I appeared regularly at Emporium, REACT's night called 'Garage' at Heaven, Tutu Tedder events at the Vauxhall Tavern and Heaven, Bagleys Warehouse in Kings Cross where I played alongside Norman Jay, The Cross, To The Manor Born, Club UK, Subterrania, Bar Rumba and The Loft.
33 I was confused and argued over the set time when they told me my set was at 2 a.m. – clubs in the UK were closed by then. I had the peak set from 2.00 to 4.00 a.m. and the club closed at 6 a.m.
34 Caroline Prothero – Artist Manager and Club Promoter extraordinaire whose credentials include the Ministry of Sound, Missdemeanours, David Guetta, Nervo and Prohibition DJ Promotions (digital).
35 Caroline also threw 'all back to mine' afterhours parties for visiting DJs back in her Nottingham student flat, working in collaboration with her flatmates James Baillie (mastermind behind Venus and The Bomb, Nottingham, and Charlie Chester from Flying Records.
36 Meg Matthews – PR and music guru, nineties Britpop and media celebrity.
37 My driver was Marvin Clarke.
38 Based in London, Wisebuddah Productions is a leading specialist in the production of sonic branding, radio imaging and jingles.
39 It is still available on Discogs and will cost you 25p. www.discogs.com/release/562413-Various-Club-Mix-96.
40 Broadsheets are large quality newspapers – *The Times*, *The Sunday Times*, the *Independent*, the *Guardian*, the *Observer*, the *Financial Times*.
41 Eddie Gordon gave me the idea of doing regular, exclusive DJ mixes containing music from the labels and sending these out to the press with the vinyl and later CD promo releases. This was not authorised and when the annual bill of duplication hit the Head of Press's desk I found myself in a huge amount of trouble. It worked but is possibly also why my expenses took so long to clear. Someone had to pay for it.
42 Britpop is short for a mid-nineties British-based music culture movement that emphasised Britishness. It produced brighter, catchier alternative rock, partly in reaction to the popularity of the darker lyrical themes of the US-led grunge music and to the UK's own shoegaze music scene.
43 Following the 1992 Castlemorton Festival, the Criminal Justice and Public Order Act (1994) was a Conservative Party initiative to curb illegal raves, free parties and festivals. Despite protests, the Labour Party abstained at the third reading and the Act was passed

Notes

into law on 3 November 1994, has never been repealed and is still being revised at the time of writing.

44 Roni Size and Represent are a Bristol based drum and bass band consisting of DJs Roni Size, DJ Krust, DJ Die and DJ Suv with musicians Onallee (singer), MC Dynamite, Si John on bass and Clive Deamer on drums. Drum and bass had never been performed live before they did it. Their album *New Forms* went five times platinum.

45 The then unknown Ralph John Perou is now known professionally as Perou and @mrperou on social media. He is a Great British fashion, portrait and music photographer who has also appeared as a judge on *Make Me a Supermodel UK* and on season 2 of Bravo TV's American *Make Me a Supermodel*.

46 *Dazed and Confused* – chic style magazine edited by Rankin.

47 Roni Size and Reprazent won the Mercury Music Prize in 1997 and were nominated 'Best British Breakthrough Act' for a BRIT Award in 1998 but lost to Stereophonics. Roni Size was also nominated in the category for Best British Producer losing out to Youth, The Verve and Chris Potter.

48 Roni Size and Reprazent's album *New Forms* beat The Chemical Brothers, Radiohead, The Prodigy and the Spice Girls.

49 The Azuli Records and Defected Records buildings faced each other on D'Arblay Street in West London.

50 Azuli Records occupied the first, second and third floor of the 29 D'Arblay Street townhouse, while Black Market Records occupied the ground floor and the basement. Both were owned by David Piccioni until Azuli went into liquidation in 2009. Defected first licensed the Azuli back catalogue and later bought the label outright in 2012. Gerry 'Goldie' McGoldrick took over the reins from David Piccioni at Black Market Records but it closed its doors in 2015.

51 Jamila Mohammed – Label Manager.

52 Christiano Spiller aka Spiller is a DJ from Venice, Italy. He is best known for his single 'Groovejet', which he recorded with Sophie Ellis Bextor. He is also possibly the tallest DJ, clocking in at 206 cm. 'Spiller from Rio' was the single that preceded 'Groovejet'.

53 Afro Medusa's 'Pasilda' was the tune of the summer, reaching number 31 in the UK singles chart in October 2000.

54 Lazy Dog was Ben Watt and Jay Hannan's Sunday night session in West London where I played as a regular guest DJ. It ran in Notting Hill Arts Club from 1998 until 2003.

55 Sebastian Doring and Thorsten Friese aka Knee Deep producers from Hamburg produced their best-known remix to date with Afro Medusa's 'Pasilda'.

Notes

56 Lenny Fontana is a disco / house music DJ from New York City, also known as Powerhouse.
57 *Miami Nice* was a TV movie / documentary created by Initial Films, directed by Angus Cameron and produced by Janie Valentine that followed four DJs around the Miami Winter Music Conference in March 2000. The DJs were MJ Cole, Roger Sanchez, Mark Jones (Wall of Sound) and myself. It has been repeated many times, last aired on Channel 5 and can still be found on IMDb.
58 Chester-born Nemone Metaxas, often billed simply as Nemone, is an English DJ, radio presenter and television presenter / producer. 6 Music and the BBC is her spiritual broadcasting home.
59 *Must Be the Music* was a house-music continuous mix compilation released in the US which had a stateside promo tour to support it.
60 Claudia Cuseta's Maxi Records / Maxi Promotions was a mythic underground independent house-music label and promotions company which hot housed the careers of Danny Tenaglia, Cevin Fisher and many more.
61 A DJ, journalist and important personality in the music industry since the 1980s, in 1998 Michael Paoletta became the Brand Marketing Editor, Dance / Electronic Music Editor, and Albums Review Editor for *Billboard Magazine*. He is now an entertainment executive; music supervisor; sync and licensing specialist; creative consultant; song plugger; and renowned specialist in pop culture.
62 8 July 2000 – Billboard's Dance Summit boasts tight line-up, top talents. Billboard conference link: http://tiny.cc/k0kzuz.
63 The Black & Blue Festival is the world's largest gay-benefit dance festival, attracting thousands of tourists to Montreal every Canadian Thanksgiving weekend and raising money for HIV/Aids and the Montreal gay community. It is organised annually by the Bad Boy Club Montréal (aka BBCM and Fondation BBCM).
64 The average UK set time was 90 minutes to two hours. Montreal minimum set time was five hours plus.
65 I appeared for the final time at the Palais des Congrès for Black & Blue 20 Years where I was body painted like Grace Jones by Zilon and DJ'ed alongside the Spanish DJs Chus and Ceballos.
66 Under the guidance of Laurent Chaumet (booker, tour manager and artist liaison) and Thibault Jardon (Directeur Artistique).
67 Karim Ech-Choaby was the Music Editor for the magazine *Technikart*, based in Bastille. He connected me to a lot of people in Paris.

Notes

68 Established in 1997, Paul and Joe is now a luxury fashion and lifestyle brand headed, as it has always been, by Sophie Mechaly.
69 Andy Wahloo is a Parisian hangout (metro Arts Et Metiers) that serves creative cocktails and champagne, with outdoor tables in a cobbled courtyard.
70 Cyber was an independent French music company and record label, mainly focused on House music. Defunct since the Parisian Techno Import shop at 6 Rue Du Commandant Lamy closed down in 2008.
71 Since the French have their own electronic music culture, stars, clubs, media and events calendar it would have to be translated into French.

3 Bad behaviour: shit shags and crap hotels

1 Grève – the least favourite word of any commuter or traveller in France – in fact in any country – means 'strike'.
2 HOME was situated in the basement of Ducie House on the corner of Ducie Street in Manchester in the nineties. This is not to be confused with HOME the arts and cultural centre that resides on First Street, also in Manchester.
3 In the nineties, sledged, spannered, hammered, mullered, twatted and fucked were slang terms for being high on ecstasy.
4 Situated in Deansgate on 4A South King St, Bar Kay was renamed South, became home to Clint Boon and finally closed its doors in June 2022.
5 India House – an Edwardian baroque packing and shipping warehouse on Whitworth Street in Manchester that was converted into an apartment block. It was home to a community of creatives (including Noel Gallagher), misfits, DJs, producers, gays and lesbians. There was always something crazy happening there.
6 In 1994 this Manchester to Brighton weekly commute took around six hours each way by train and was gruelling. In 2001 Virgin Trains (established in 1997) bought 53 class 390 high speed Pendolino trains and introduced them in the UK, linking cities like London, Manchester, Birmingham and Glasgow, making the daily commute feasible.
7 On 3 August 1994 the IRA had claimed responsibility for the seaside bicycle bombs which had been planted to mark the twenty-fifth anniversary of the British troops' arrival in Northern Ireland. The Brighton bomb had been located and defused but the Bognor bomb detonated destroying fifteen shops and cars.

Notes

8   Caner is a slang term for a drug user who takes / thrashes a lot of drugs.
9   1998 – Andy Parfitt was the Radio 1 Controller.
10 Amnesia – nightclub in Ibiza.
11 Anne Marie Bigby was our Promotions Manager and marketing specialist.
12 Where's Kevin? – reference to Macaulay Culkin's character in the 1990 Hollywood blockbuster movie *Home Alone*.
13 *Hierbas* is an aniseed-flavoured liqueur particular to the Balearic Islands, served as an after-dinner digestive over ice or as a 'chupito' shot. When drunk to excess it gives the most horrendous hangover.
14 *Lumumba* was the hype nineties Spanish chocolate milk and brandy / amaretto drink to order.
15 MDMA is the acronym for the compound 3,4-Methylenedioxy methamphetamine, more commonly known as ecstasy when in pill form.
16 *The Guardian*, 'Annie Nightingale: Radio 1's first female DJ and Caner of the Year 2001', Caroline Sullivan, 2015.
17 From my Director of A&R and Promotions chair at Azuli Records.
18 Joey Negro – now known as Dave Lee, Z Records owner and artist and a legendary international DJ / producer.
19 AKA was the bar adjoining Mr C and Layo Paskin's club called 'The End' in West London.
20 David Banner – The Incredible Hulk.
21 Stereo is a legendary nightclub and afterhours club in Montreal, founded in 1998 by Angel Moraes (RIP). It has a bespoke, high-end soundsystem and is celebrated for house and techno music.
22 'Piscines' are double balloon glasses of champagne served with ice.
23 'Coup d'un soir' – one night stand.
24 'J'ai très mal au ventre' translates as 'I feel sick' or 'I have a bad stomach ache' – a weak excuse but relatively accurate.
25 The Virgin Megastore no longer exists or operates at this location on the Champs Élysées. It declared itself insolvent in 2013 with debts of £223m due to consumer trends moving towards online and digital purchases of music and film. The site was purchased by Galeries Lafayette and the new store with its breath-taking design by Danish Architect Bjarke Ingels, was opened in March 2019. https://fashionunited.uk/news/retail/in-pictures-galeries-lafayette-to-open-new-champs-elysees-flagship-this-week/2019032642369.
26 Translates as someone who does things in bad faith, is evil or disrespectful.

Notes

4 FAQs (female asked questions)

1 London born, Manchester based DJ, producer, label owner and Ninja Tunes recording artist, Anz curated the 'Normal Not Novelty' workshops for Red Bull.
2 Red Bull – Normal Not Novelty #NormalNotNovelty was a monthly workshop which invited women to build lasting networks in the music industry. It was open to female-identifying DJs, sound engineers, producers and vocalists from all musical tastes and backgrounds.
3 1978–93, the Hulme Crescents was the largest public housing development in Europe. In 1984, by then deemed disastrous and uninhabitable and lacking the budget to demolish, Manchester City Council stopped charging tenants rent and supplied electricity for those who stayed. The Crescents became an eclectic home to subcultures, creatives, bohemians, drug dealers, criminals and squatters. The illegal nightclub The Kitchen was based here. They were demolished in 1993.
4 Michelle Mangan played at the Lesbian Summer of Love for Lucy Scher, had spots on the main floor for the first three Flesh parties and played on Tuesdays at the Number 1 Club in Manchester.
5 Phillipa Jarman is one of the founders of Piccadilly Records – one of the longest standing and most revered vinyl emporiums in Manchester.
6 I DJ'ed with Paula and Tabs at Michael Anthony Barnes-Wynter's 'Hoochie Coochie' club night at Oscars and The State in Manchester.
7 Body and Soul took place Sundays weekly at Club Vinyl in Tribeca NYC featuring resident DJs Danny Krivit, François K and Joaquin 'Joe' Claussell.
8 Jackie Christie came to notoriety through MTV's 'The Grind', through her residencies at The Limelight and Studio 54 and the *Hard and Tasty Beats* compilations on New York label Nervous Records.
9 Cheryl Robson was the ground-breaking female head of A&R at Virgin Records' sister label Innocent. The roster included top selling albums from Billie (Piper) and Martine McCutcheon. www.theguardian.com/world/1999/apr/15/gender.uk1.
10 Nancy Berry – Executive Vice President of Virgin Group Worldwide.
11 Leroy Richardson – Haçienda Bar Manager and Licensee / Dry Bar 201 Manager and longest-serving member of staff.

Notes

12 Judy Griffith is the Programming and Partnerships Director at Fabric in London. At the time of writing, Fabric is one of the longest-standing nightclubs in London's nightlife history (next to the Ministry of Sound) and in the world. It still operates on the original site in Farringdon.
13 Designer / stylist Patricia Fields had House of Fields.
14 Owned and operated by the BBC, 1Xtra is the digital sister station to Radio 1, broadcasting Black music, hip hop, soul and R&B.
15 Jaguar – BBC Introducing Dance presenter, Mixmag Weekend Editor, Utopia Talks, BEMA.
16 Erica McKoy is a broadcaster, presenter, audio producer and a DJ. She presented the *Breakfast Show* on Gilles Peterson's Worldwide FM throughout lockdown.
17 Transmission Roundhouse Radio Station is a socially engaged podcast platform powered by the Roundhouse, a home for niche, innovative and ground-breaking audio-led content that champions the voices of underrepresented young creatives.
18 The Lady Miss Kier Kirby – singer / songwriter of Deee-Lite, DJ, designer, fashion icon, dancer and activist.
19 Annie Nightingale, *Hey Hi Hello*, Sheryl Garratt, *Adventures In Wonderland*, Miki Berenyi, *Fingers Crossed: How Music Saved Me from Success*, Audrey Golden, *I Thought I Heard You Speak: The Women of Factory* and Emma Warren *Dance Your Way Home: A Journey Through the Dancefloor*.
20 Myalgic encephalomyelitis / chronic fatigue syndrome is a serious, long-term illness that affects many body systems.
21 Legend: Annie Mac is leaving BBC1 after 17 years, BBC News, 20 April 2021. www.bbc.co.uk/news/newsbeat-56814062.
22 DJ Lottie – globe-trotting international DJ / producer and Radio 1 presenter cites motherhood, parenting and childcare issues as hurdles in her DJ career. www.decodedmagazine.com/lottie-talks-music-parenting-infamous-Haçienda.
23 Amanda Spielman speech – 2022 National Children and Adult Services Conference. www.gov.uk/government/speeches/amanda-spielmans-speech-at-the-2022-national-children-and-adult-services-conference.
24 Madonna acceptance speech – Billboard Women In Music Awards 2016. https://twitter.com/billboard/status/808522434127294465?s=20&t=bPqtzrFcYD4rh9OY2Refog.
25 *New York Times* – Honey Dijon Steps Up From Dance Music's Underground, Rich Juzwiak 22 November 2022. www.nytimes.com/2022/11/22/arts/music/honey-dijon-black-girl-magic.html.

Notes

26 Bloomberg – UK Gender Pay Gap Persists after Five years of Disclosure. 31 March 2022.
27 Kamila Rymajdo – A Barrier to Being Seen: Ageism and Sexism Intersect on the Dancefloor. https://ra.co/features/3930.
28 'We Can Be in Bed by 1am – Amazing': Veteran DJ Annie Mac's New Clubbing Venture Hits the Spot – Alexandra Topping, the *Guardian* 21 May 2022. www.theguardian.com/tv-and-radio/2022/may/21/we-can-be-in-bed-by-1am-amazing-veteran-DJ-annie-macs-new-clubbing-venture-hits-the-spot.

5 How to kill a DJ

1 Cover feature – Todd Edwards, *DJ Magazine*, June 2021.
2 Flesh at the Haçienda and Paradise Factory resident DJ and Graphic Designer Dave Kendrick is the mind behind Castrocorp – Subverting Pixels since 2001 (https://castrocorp.co.uk). Clients include Defected Records, Holly Johnson, Nick Helm, D:Vision and Brighton and Hove Pride.
3 Tom Anderson – the founder of Myspace was everybody's first friend.
4 The iPhone App Store opened on 10 July 2008.
5 Forerunner to the BBC Red Button, Ceefax 'seeing facts' was established in 1972 and had its last transmission in 2012. https://pastandpresent.org.uk/digital-narratives-of-the-1990s.
6 Sheryl Garratt at *The Face*, Avril Mair at *i-D*, June Joseph, Emma Warren, Sarah Champion, Sharon O Connell at *Melody Maker*, Helene Stokes and Claire Hughes at *DJ Magazine*.
7 Women and the UK Music Press – Cazz Blaze 2012, The F Word. https://thefword.org.uk/2012/02/women_and_the_music_press.
8 50 Greatest Music Books – *Observer Monthly*. www.theguardian.com/observer/omm/story/0,,1797454,00.html.
9 Doug Young – previously Publishing Director at Penguin Random House and now Associate Agent at Pew Literary Agency.
10 Sheryl Garratt, *Adventures in Wonderland: Decade of Club Culture*.
11 *Mixmag* – Blackout feature written by Jaguar. https://mixmag.net/feature/the-unsung-black-women-pioneers-of-house-music.
12 *DJ Magazine* – Dance Music Is Black Music issue (Dec 2020). Also read Diversity and Equality Report Q2 2022. https://DJmag.com/news/DJ-mag-diversity-equality-report-q2–2022.
13 John Burgess and Paul Benney are responsible for creating and editing the irreverent underground music fanzine / magazine *Jockey Slut* (1993–99), the 'Bugged Out' parties (celebrating their twenty-fifth anniversary in 2023) and the twice-yearly title *Disco Pogo* in 2022.

Notes

6 Sane as it ever was

1. Nadine Noor and Skye Barr founded Pxssy Palace (2015), a club night that prioritises people of colour from marginalised genders and sexualities. Pxssy Palace does vital community work raising money for LGBTQ+ youth, helping trans femmes of colour stay safe, and enraging cis straight white men.
2. Sacha Lord, Night Time Economy Adviser for Greater Manchester Combined Authority appointed by Mayor Andy Burnham. Co-founder and Director of the Warehouse Project and Parklife.
3. Andy Burnham, Mayor of Greater Manchester Combined Authority.
4. The Met in Bury is an independent arts and entertainment venue run by Bury Metropolitan Arts Association and situated in Bury, North Manchester. https://themet.org.uk.
5. Mary Ellen McTague – chef, writer and CSO / founder of the non-profit chef and restaurant collective 'Eat Well MCR'.
6. Fred Again and The Blessed Madonna, 'Marea (We've Lost Dancing)'. https://youtu.be/yMJswjcD8Fg.
7. Sally Anne Gross and George Musgrave, *Can Music Make You Sick?* In this important book, Sally Anne Gross and George Musgrave investigate the relationship between the wellbeing music brings to society and the wellbeing of those who create. It's a much-needed reality check, de-glamorising the romantic image of the tortured artist. https://westminsterresearch.westminster.ac.uk/item/v109w/can-music-make-you-sick-measuring-the-price-of-musical-ambition.

7 Lifetime VIP: a manifesto

1. 'Undoing Death's Work: The Role of Women In 18th–20th Century Literature' was my 1994 University thesis.
2. Excerpt of Mary Walker's poem 'Be Not Silent', 2019. Reproduced with permission of the author. See her website at www.marywalker.co.nz.
3. Naomi Pohl was elected the first female General Secretary of the Musicians' Union since the union's creation in 1893.
4. 'Progressing Gender Representation in UK Dance Music', published by the Jaguar Foundation, funded by Sony Music's Social Justice Fund. www.sonymusic.co.uk/report-exploring-gender-representation-in-uk-dance-music-published-by-the-jaguar-foundation-funded-by-sony-musics-social-justice-fund.

Index

Page numbers in **bold** refer to illustrations

A Bit Ginger Productions 19, 29–30, 225n.13
acid house 13
ACID HOUSE **164**
Adams, Oleta 43–44
Adekoya, Tunde 196
Adele 18–19, 23–24, 25
Adeva 26
AFRODEUTSCHE 166
Afro Medusa, 'Pasilda' 57
ageing and ageism 111, 114–118
Aids crisis 3
Albert's Schloss 7, 142, 143, 150
Alexandra Palace 85–86
All Back to Minehead **181**
Amsterdam 121–122
Anderton, James 19–20
Angelou, Maya 118
Another Late Night 57
Anz 11, 97, 126, 201, 214, 236n.1
Archives, Nia 197
Arrojo, Nick 35
Auburn, Rachel 25
Avis-Ward, Daisy 198
Azuli Presents Choice 57
Azuli Presents Space 58
Azuli Records 6, 55, 56–58, **65**, 84–85

BaadAsss TV (TV programme) 42
Baduel, Antoine 137
Bagehot, Walter 161
Ball, Graham 48
Ball, Zoe 82
Bar Kay 32
Barnes-Wynter, Michael 33–34
Bartlett, Dawn 42
BBC internship programme 102, 106
BB Supernature 117
Beams, The **180**
Beatnik, Nikki 117
Bee, Sophie 150–152, 153, 226n.26
Bell, Janet 55
BEMA 198
Benjamin, Baroness Floella 8–9, 226n.16
Benjamin, Kim 107
Benney, Paul 135–136

240

Index

Berry, Nancy 99
Beyoncé 3
Bibby, Jeff 33–34
Bigby, Anne Marie **66**, 83, 143, **171**
Billboard Music Conference 59
Black & Blue Festival 59, 86–87
Black Artist Database 191, 196, 198–200, 204
Black History Month 196
Black Lives Matter 133
Blackness 8, 42, 135, 187
Black press, the 50
Black Riot Records 110
Blair, Tony 51
Blessed Madonna, The 14, 102–103, 153
Bloxham, Tom 74–75
Boiler Room 146–147
Bowery, Leigh 26
Boy George 37–38, 48
#breakthebias 10
Breeze, Gina 147, 217
Brewster, Bill 11, 58, 129–130, 131, 196, 226n.22
Brierly, Alex 45
Brighton 38, 39–40, 80, 81, 98, 136, 154–155, 224n.14, 228n.21, 234n.6, 235n.7, 238n.2
Britpop 51
BRITS school 107
Brooks, Gareth 148
Broughton, Frank 2, 11, 129–130, 187, 131, 187, 196, 224n.3, 226n.21
Brown, Pam 107
Burdess, Paula 76–77, 95, **164**
Burgess, John 135–136
Burnham, Andy 148
Bushell, Ian 19
Bushell, Simon 28–29, 36

Cadoux, Alice 47
Callier, Terry 51, 52–53, 54
Campbell, Joseph 190
cancel culture 124
caner culture 82–87
Can't Get High Without You (Joey Negro) 84
Carr, Malaika 111–112
Carr, Marcia 8, 45–47, 96, 97, 108, 111–112, 114–115
Carroll, Andy 83
Castrocorp 124–125
Channel 4 120
Chapman, Sarah 98
Christie, Jackie 98
Claridge's Hotel 43–44
Clayton, John 4
Club Mix 96 X 49
Coe, Fiona 61
Colmar 88
Commission on Race and Ethnic Disparities 9
Cons, Paul 5, 19, 20–22, 23, 24, 25, 27–28, 29–30, 31, 32, 74–75, 79–80, 225n.13, 227n.4, 227n.5
Covid 19 pandemic and lockdown
  events affected by lockdown 153–160
  lessons learned 203, 205
  lockdown initiatives 133, 134, 148, 149, **172–175**, 217, 237
  overview of the pandemic 11, 12, 13
  pandemic aftershocks 110, 191, 202
  quarantine 16
  reality of covid 22, 141–144, 151–155, 198, 200
  self care through lockdown 161, 162, 184
Crago, Jojo 150

Index

Crank, Lee 147
Crawford, Sarah Jane 102, 106
Criminal Justice Bill 51
crutches 92–93
Cunningham, Claud 98
Cuseta, Claudia 58, 101–102, 107, 205

Danger, Dulcie 6, 40, 98, 103, 136, 154, 207, 225n.14, 228n.1
Dangerously, Johnny 63
Davies, Nicola **178**, 198
Dazed and Confused 52, 53
Defected Records 55–56, 60
Def, Paolo 47
De Sousa, Nick 7
Destroy 26
Dick Whittington syndrome 136
difference, stigma of 95–96
Dijon, Honey 14, 115
Disco Pogo 135–136, 196
diversity 189–190
Divine David 26
DJ Colleen 'Cosmo' Murphy 8, 89, 103, 113, 117, 189
DJ death 119–124, 136–141
DJ Lottie 59, 60, 113
DJ Magazine 27, 133, 134–135, 188, 196, 209
DJ Michelle 98
DJ Paulette **63–71**, **164**, **165**, **167–175**
   activism 37–38
   career beginnings 5–7, 16–22
   celebrity 37–38
   divorce 2, 30–32, 38
   DJ death 119–124, 136–141
   early music industry experience 3–5
   fight for recognition 29
   first Club Mix compilation 49
   first DJ gig 18–19
   Flesh residency 20–32
   growth 185
   learns how to DJ 20–32
   Lifetime Achievement Award 14, 208–209
   lockdown radio mixes 147–150
   marriage 2, 22
   mental health struggles 12, 32
   move to London 5–6, 80–81
   move to Paris 60
   New York quarantine 52–53
   online presence 124–128
   persona 35–36
   perspective 3
   recommendation for change 184–196
   siblings 95
   as singer 5
   support network 14
   wedge compression fracture 143
   writing choices 130–131
Douglas, Gavin 99
Douglas, Wendy 40–41, 42, **66**
dreams 188–189
drugs and drug abuse 75–78, 78, 80, 82–87, 91–93, 119–120
Dunmore, Simon 55, 142, 227n.9
Dunne, David 60, 121

Earl Gateshead 103
Ech-Choaby, Karim 60
editorial bias 11, 109
Edwards, Todd 120
Einstein, Albert 193
Elizabeth II, Queen 3, 11
equality 105
Ericsson 194
Escape to Freight Island project 150, 153
Evans, Chris 3–4

Index

Fabric 108
Fac 51 5
The Face 52–53
Facebook 125
Ferdinand, Kay 196, 198–200
Finkelstein, Mark 100
Finlay, Blanche 80, 94–95, **164**
Finlayson, Walter George **64, 163**
Fitzgerald, Muff 54
Flesh 5, 20–32, 98
Fletcher, Paul 155–158, 162
Floyd, George, murder of 133, 190
Fontana, Lenny 58
4Hero 51, 54
Four Women project **166**
Fox, Stephanie 148
France 87–91, 137–138
Fred Again 153
Freud, Sigmund 2
Funk Butcher 133–134, 190
Future Music 52–53

Gallagher, Rob 1
Garner, Tristan 90–91
Garratt, Sheryl 130
Gary (friend of author) 75, 80–81
gatekeepers, male 128–133
Gay Pride 154–155
gender 95–97, 115–117
Glastonbury Festival 3
Glory Hole, The 32, 79–80
Gordon, Eddie 42, 43, 49, 54, 83
Gou, Peggy 14
Granada TV 36–37
Gray, Peter 35
Griffith, Judy 8, 98, 100–101, 108, 111, 237n.12
Gruissan 89–90
Guetta, David 88

Haçienda, the 4, 19–22, 34, 149–150, 155–158, **174, 180,** 203
Flesh 5, 20–32, 98
the Pussy Parlour 24, 25, 31–32
Haji, Seamus 55
Hargreaves, Roger, *Little Miss Star* 184–185
Haslam, Dave 11, 133
Heaven 38
hidden histories 10, 130, 133, 186
Hinds, Colin 184–185
Hinton, Jeffrey 25
Hobbs, Mary Anne 108
Hogg, Pam 26
HOME 75–78
Homebird **169**
homophobia 36, 121, 188
Hoochie Coochie 33–34
Hook, Peter 5, 11, 20–21, 128–129, 149, 202
Hopper, Jeannie 98
House of Fields 101
Howard, Luke 5, 25–26

I'Anson, Lisa 82
Ibiza 7, 62, **65,** 82, 82–84, 91–92, 122
Ice-T 42
inclusion 189–190
Industria 47
Instagram 160
Internet, the 46–47, 120, 124–128
the *i* (newspaper) 10
It Girl 40

Jackson, Elton 34–35
Jacobs, Dani 4
Jaguar 8, 11, 102–103, 106, 108, 133–134, 161, **178,** 189, 197–198, 237n.15, 238n.11

Index

Jaguar Foundation 197, 239n.4
Jamz Supernova 8, 11, 99, 102, 104, 107, 113–114, 127, 189, 197
Jarman, Phillipa 98
Jay, Norman 40, 83, 139, 140
Judge Jules 42–43, 83
Juice (TV show) 36–37, **63**, 75–78
Jung, Carl 187

Kath 5, 28, 32, 80, 97, 98, 103, 112, 136, 207, 225n.13
Kelly, Christopher 37
Kempadoo, Janine 102
Kemp, Paul 154
Kervorkian, François 103
Khan, Nadia 194
Kimpton Clock Tower Hotel 16
King, Martin Luther, Jr 140, 208
Kingsley, Gavin 60, 121
Kirby, Kier 107
Knott, Gordon 27
Kurz, Wayne 38

La Bellevilloise, Paris 1
Ladybeige, Rina 112
La Fête de la Musique and Technoparade 90–91
La India 53
Laidback Luke 2
Lakuti 98, 103, 108, 109, 115, 117–118, 195
Lamarr, Kendrick 3
Lamb 42
Lennox, Tim 28
Lilley, Patrick 25
Lin 28
Lions, Charlotte 60, 61
literature 128–136
Little Simz 3
Liverpool 28
Loben, Carl 11, 128, 132, 134–135

London 5–6, 39–42, 80–81, 119–121, 136–137, 142
London Pride 3
Loose 28
Lord, Sacha 148–150, 156, 162
Lorde, Audre 185, 188
Loud and Proud (radio programme) 37–38
Lynch, Monica 101

Mac, Annie vii–viii, 14, 99, 102, 112–113, 116–117, 117
McCall, Davina 48
McCormack, Jo 99
Machin, Steve 28–29
McHugh, Kevin 101
McKenzie, Donna 103
McKenzie, Roger 103
McKoy, Erica 11, 106, 158
McLeod, Neil 142
McVey, Lynn 98
Madonna 2, 115
Manchester 3–5, 7, 13, 16–22, 32–37, 80, 94, 97–98, 106, 107, 123, 143, 155–158, 187, 196
Manchester Evening News 4
Mancuso, David 103
Manifesto Records 43
Martin, Paul 42, 54, 55
Massey, Chris 109–110, 147, **168**
Masters at Work 52
Masters, James 155
Matthews, Ang 5, 99
Matthews, Meg 47
Maurel, Henri 137, 137–138
Maxi Records 101–102
May, Derrick 130
Melody Maker 132
Menard, Ludovic 61, 137
Mercer, Kas 42, 43
Mercury Music Prize 54
Mercury Records 6, 42–44, 49–55, 83

Index

Metaxas, Nemone 58
Miami Nice 58
Ministry of Sound 6, 47–49, 57, 60, 62, 120–121, 124, 203
Missdemeanours 84, 113
Mission Mars 143, 150
Mistajam 202
Mix Club 6
Mixmag 82, 133–134, **178**, 188
Mixmag Update 41
Mohammed, Jamila 56, 232n.51
Monteco, Fafa 60
Montreal 86–87
Moovin Festival 155–156
motherhood 111–114
M-People 26
Mr Mike 47
Mulraine, Ruby 102
Music Week Press Award 54
Must Be the Music 58
Muzik Magazine 52, 82, 84
Myspace 125

Negro, Joey 84, 124
Nervous Records 58–59
Neville, Luke 83
Newley, Tara **63**
New York 21, 25–26, 52–53
New York Times 115
Neye, Janine 41
Nightingale, Annie 84, 85
NIKS 8, 11, 189, 191, 193, 196, 198, 200, 204
NME 195
Noor, Nadine 146, 195, 201
NorthSouth 29
Number 1 Club 5, 17–19, 31

Oliver, Andi 42
Oliviera, Sam 147
Oscars 80
Ovenden, Mark 37, 60, 121

PACE (Police and Criminal Evidence Act, 1984) 33
Paoletta, Michael 53
Parfitt, Andy 82
Paris 1, 6, 39, 60, 61–62, **67**, **70**, 90–91
Parklife 21 149–150
'Paulette Presents Together' 153, **176**
Perou, Ralph 52
Perusse, David 59
Peterson, Gilles 1, 6, 40, 40–41, 42, 54, 55, 136, **171**, 196, 207, 208, 226n.26, 237n.16
Pet Shop Boys 26
Phillips, Dom 49, 203–204
PhutureTrax Management 45, 47
Piccadilly Radio 261 3–4
Piccioni, David 6, 55, 56–57, 58, **65**
Pizarro, Gladys 99–101, 207
Pohl, Naomi 194, 200–201, 203
Poll Tax 3
Polygram 6
Portugal 47
Princess Julia 25, 48
Prothero, Caroline 6, 47–48, 84, 99, 113, 205, 227n.9, 231n.34
Pxxssy Palace trans-body positive collective 201

Q Magazine 53
Queen Club 7
Queer Academy 28
queer culture, explosion of 36–37
Queer Nation, London 25–26

racism 8–9, 121, 124, 159, 188
Radio 1 Weekend 82
Radio FG 7, 137–138

Index

Rapido TV 42
Rashford, Marcus 9
REACT 38
Rebelle, Josey 126
recession, 1992 3
Reprazent 6, 51–52, 53–54, 99
representation 188
Resident Advisor 157
Richardson, Leroy 33, 99
Roberts, Juliet 26
Roberts, Pops **182**, 210
Robson, Cheryl 99
Roger, Rachel 147
role models and mentors 8–10, 95–105, 189
Rollins, Sean 1
Rothery, Matthew 112
Rousse, Caroline 59
Ryan, Matt 31, 80
Rymajdo, Kamila 10, 115–116, 117, 196, 216, 226n.20, 238n.27

Samrai, Balraj 196
Sanchez, Roger 52, 78
Saturday Express 3–4
Saunderson, Kevin 130
Sayed, Bee 41
Scher, Lucy 19, 21, 22, 23, 24, 25, 27–28, 29–30, 31, 32, 48, 74–75, 79–80, 103, 227n.4, 236n.4
Schneider, Anja 117
Section 28 3, 36
Seen 196
sexism 9, 121, 188
Share The Fall EP (Roni Size and Reprazent) 51–52
Sharp, Robert 60
Shelter, The 25–26
Sherelle 11, 136, **183**, 196, 201
'Sheroes' 109–110
Shogbola, Hannah 198

Sinclair, Didier 60, 61, 137
Sinclar, Bob 90–91
sisterly solidarity 108
Size, Roni 6, 51–52, 54, **64**
Smokin Jo 44, 130
social media 124–128, 160–161
Solveig, Martin 60
Sony Music Social Justice Fund 197
Soundcloud 11, 126
Sound Factory, The 25–26
Soundhouse Session 45–47
Southport Weekender 78–79
So What 29
Space Ibiza 122
speaking out 203–204
Spirit, Chris 98
Star, Heléna 198
Starr, Edwin **65**
Stream GM 148–149
streaming services 28
stress 159
Strictly Rhythm 99–101, 227n.9
SUS laws 3, 19, 33
Sweeney, Sarah 117

Take That 26
Talkin' Loud 51
Tash LC 97
Terry, Todd 78, 79, 122
That's How It Is 41
Thompson, Andy 42
tokenism 105
Tong, Pete 42, 54
training 20–30, 105–108
Transmission Roundhouse Radio Station 106
travel 72–74
Trax, Nicky 45, 47
Tribal Gathering 53
truth, finding 204
Twitter 160

Index

UK Rumbal 45

Valentine, Janie 36
Virgin Records 99
visibility 128–136, 185–187, 188

Wahloo, Andy 61
Walker, Mary 192
Walther, Daniel 47
Want, Becky 3–4
wellness 160–161
We Out Here Festival **171**
Westbrook, Daniella 82
Westwood, Vivienne 26
Whatmough, Chris 4
whitewashing 11

Wilcox, Ben 41
Wilkinson, Mark 57
Williams, Demetrius 121
Williams, Kevin 58, 59
Winter Music Conference 59, 101–102
women
　status of 108–118
　support 193
　visibility 128–136, 185–187, 188
Worldwide FM 158–159

Young, Doug 129

Zap Club 6, 38, 39–40, 48